GENERATION
~ TO ~
GENERATION

Passing on a Legacy of Faith to Our Children

ALSO BY AUTHOR

Holy Land Reflections:
A Collection of Inspirational Insights from Israel

Spiritual Cooking with Yael

YAEL ECKSTEIN

FOREWORD BY DR. PAT ROBERTSON
AND GORDON ROBERTSON

GENERATION
~TO~
GENERATION

Passing on a Legacy of Faith to Our Children

International Fellowship
of Christians and Jews®

Cover and interior design by MarketOne Consultants, Fort Worth, Texas
Cover photo image: Shutterstock
Inside cover photo of Rabbi Yechiel Eckstein and Yael Eckstein by Olivier Fitoussi
IFCJ Project Staff: Caleb Burroughs, David Kuner, Yonit Rothchild, and Betsy Schmitt
Published by the International Fellowship of Christians & Jews, Inc. with offices in Canada, Israel,
South Korea, and the United States.

ISBN 978-0-9835327-6-7
First Printing: 2020

With eternal gratitude to God for blessing me with the perfect parents who taught me the way I should go.

CONTENTS

FOREWORD

When a young Orthodox Rabbi began his visionary work in 1983 building bridges of understanding between Christians and Jews, it was Dr. Pat Robertson, president of CBN and Regent University, who was one of the first Christian leaders to step forward to embrace Rabbi Yechiel Eckstein's work. Following Rabbi Eckstein's untimely death in 2019, his daughter Yael Eckstein stood at the helm of the organization the Rabbi founded, the International Fellowship of Christians and Jews, *as its new president. And it was Dr. Robertson's son, Gordon Robertson, who stepped forward to offer his support. Father and son. Father and daughter. Each represents a link in the chain of faith that stretches from generation to generation, and extends that legacy of faith beyond the boundaries of time and space for generations to come.*

I was privileged to know and to support an extraordinary man, Yechiel Eckstein. Yechiel was an Orthodox Rabbi who realized that building bridges between Christians and Jews was a worthy center for a lifetime work.

After the horrors of the Holocaust and the refusal of some Christian groups to intervene, there arose in the Jewish community a profound aversion to Christians. Yet in the modern-day evangelical church, there is a profound love of Israel and Jewish causes.

Yechiel Eckstein saw beyond the prejudices of his day to build a fellowship which has brought tens of millions of dollars in relief to beleaguered Holocaust survivors and needy Jews in Israel and around the world that springs forth from the love which evangelical Christians have for Israel.

The work of the *International Fellowship of Christians and Jews* is indeed profound, and I am delighted that Yechiel's daughter, Yael, is carrying on the work of her father. I know that good things are still to come in his memory and as his legacy.

Pat Robertson
Founder/Chairman
The Christian Broadcasting Network, Inc.

Have you ever wondered why God chose Abraham? Genesis 18:19 gives us the answer: "*For I have known him, in order that he may command his children and his household after him, that they keep the way of the LORD, to do righteousness and justice, that the LORD may bring to Abraham what He has spoken to him*" (NKJV). The "*keeping of the way of the LORD*" is not only the secret to Abraham being chosen; it is also the secret to the survival of Judaism. Even without dwelling in their homeland for more than 2,000 years, the Jewish people have survived. No other nation on earth has retained their culture and their faith for 4,000 years.

God is the God of generations, the God of Abraham, Isaac, and Jacob, and this pattern of generations has been repeated since Abraham to the present day. The faith of our fathers is a legacy that requires each generation to keep the way of the Lord. Within the Jewish family, each generation plays a role in observance in the home, from the youngest asking questions at the *seder*, to the mother lighting candles, to the grandfather and father giving the blessing over the children on the Sabbath. Judaism is not just observed in the synagogue, it is primarily observed in the home, and each member of the family is a participant.

In today's world, we live in a culture that is increasingly intolerant of belief, particularly belief in a Judeo-Christian worldview, and in commandments to obey. For years, I have longed for a book, a manual, that could be used by Christian families to transmit a living faith through the generations even while living in a hostile culture. Yael Eckstein has given us that book.

May you study it, may you adopt it, and more importantly, may you do what is written here. If you do, you will find that as we keep our faith, our faith will in turn keep us.

Gordon Robertson
President and CEO
The Christian Broadcasting Network, Inc.

INTRODUCTION

Let each generation tell its children of your mighty acts;
let them proclaim your power. — PSALM 145:4, NLT

On February 6, 2019, my life changed forever with one phone call. I had just returned from a family vacation when I received the news that my Abba, my father, Rabbi Yechiel Eckstein, had unexpectedly and tragically passed away at age 67. In the blink of an eye, I had lost my father, my mentor, and my role model.

INSPIRED BY MY FATHER'S WORK AND VISION IN FOUNDING THE *International Fellowship of Christians and Jews*, I had decided to follow in his footsteps, dedicating my life, as he had, to bringing Christians and Jews together and helping Jewish people in need in Israel and around the world. Just months earlier, *The Fellowship*'s Board of Directors had named me President-elect to take up my father's mantle once he retired in three years. I had been blessed to work alongside my father since 2005, taking in his vision, his direction, and more recently, taking on more of the day-to-day duties of running the organization. However, the plan had always been for him to be by my side, guiding me through the transition. Now, bereft and devastated, I faced an unknown future on unfamiliar terrain.

Yet, in those difficult days following my father's passing, what became increasingly clear to me was that he had been preparing me for this very moment my entire life. Not only had he begun training me for running the largest nonprofit humanitarian organization in Israel, more importantly, he had been instilling in me from my childhood the foundational values I would need to navigate this world and make it a better place. My father had left me a legacy of faith.

As renowned Christian preacher Billy Graham said, "The greatest legacy one can pass on to one's children and grandchildren is not money or other material things accumulated in one's life, but rather a legacy of character and faith." In Judaism, we refer to this as *l'dor v'dor*, which literally means "from generation to generation." We pass down our faith to the next generation not just through formal religious training, but through the holy observances, the rituals, and the traditions that happen within the life of the family. I learned the importance of setting priorities and putting God first through the weekly observance of *Shabbat*. I learned the value of asking questions and seeking wisdom as my family gathered around the *seder* table for Passover. Each holiday that we observed throughout the year, and each tradition that we followed — from the *tzedakah* (charity) box we kept in the kitchen to the reciting of blessings before and after every meal — were opportunities for my mother and father to reinforce the fundamental values of hope, gratitude, generosity, courage, faith, and forgiveness. It is these same values that my husband and I are now teaching and passing on to our four children. I know this brought great pride to my father as he watched his grandchildren being raised with those same values and with so much love for God.

When he founded *The Fellowship* in 1983, my father believed that it was this common ground, this commitment to faith and instilling these fundamental values in our children, that both Christians and Jews shared. He dedicated his life to building bridges of understanding between Christians and Jews. As more and more Christians began exploring the Jewish roots of their faith, he shared with them how the apostle Paul in Romans 11 taught that Christians have been grafted onto the rich olive tree of Israel. It is with his vision in mind that I write this book and invite you to take this journey of faith with me.

In the pages of this book, we will explore holy observances of the Jewish year and the key value it reinforces, through the teachings I learned at my father's feet, and how my husband and I now incorporate those teachings into our own family. In addition, after each chapter, we have provided a section just for you with information on how the observance is mentioned in the Christian Bible, along with questions and Bible stories to discuss with your family, and a selection of Bible verses to memorize that emphasize a key value. My prayer is that you, too, will be inspired and encouraged as you pass on your faith and train your children for lives of godliness.

Finally, this book is a tribute to my father, in deep gratitude for his love and for his legacy. Shortly before he passed away, my father gave me his blessing in preparation for the day I would assume the duties as president. He said to me then, "This is the prayer I've recited over you every Friday night on *Shabbat* since you were born: May the Lord bless you like our mothers Sarah, Rebekah, Rachel, and Leah. May the Lord bless you and watch over you. May He let His light shine upon you and be gracious unto you. May He lift up His countenance unto you and grant you *shalom*, peace. This is my blessing to you, that your life with your family, with your children, and your calling be filled with love and meaning."

These are the words that I have carried in my heart since that darkest day, and which have enabled me to carry on my father's legacy and pass it on to my own children. Thank you, *Abba*. I love you always.

Yael Eckstein

Yael Eckstein
Fellowship President & CEO

לְדוֹר וָדוֹר

L'DOR V'DOR

OVERVIEW

TEACHING OUR CHILDREN

These commandments that I give you today are to be on
your hearts. Impress them on your children. Talk about
them when you sit at home and when you walk along the
road, when you lie down and when you get up.

— DEUTERONOMY 6:6-7

Start children off on the way they should go,
and even when they are old they will not turn from it.

— PROVERBS 22:6

21

"For four thousand years our people survived because in every generation, Jews made it their highest priority to hand their faith on to their children. They sanctified marriage. They consecrated the Jewish home. They built schools and houses of study. They saw education as the conversation between the generations."

— *Lord Rabbi Jonathan Sacks, former Chief Rabbi of Great Britain*

I AM LIVING THE JEWISH DREAM. FOR NEARLY TWO THOUSAND years, since the destruction of the Holy Temple in Jerusalem and the expulsion of the Jewish people from Israel, my people have prayed and hoped for one thing, "to be a free people in our own land" (*Hatikvah*, Israel's national anthem). In 2005, my husband and I decided to realize that dream of returning to Israel and living in the Holy Land. Today, I am blessed to raise my family in our biblical homeland.

But I grew up living the American dream. I was born and raised in Chicago, Illinois, where I enjoyed the freedom and opportunities that this great country provided for my family. My parents sent me to an outstanding Jewish school where I received an excellent education, and our family was part of an active and vibrant Jewish community. We spent our weekends at the synagogue, and our lives revolved around the Jewish calendar and lifecycle events. We lit our Sabbath candles every Friday, we built our *sukkah* in the backyard during *Sukkot*, we gathered with family and friends around the *seder* table to celebrate Passover. My childhood is filled with the memories of these *moadim*, "appointed times," where the stories of our faith were shared, and the fundamental values of Judaism were reinforced and celebrated.

It was only when I was older that I understood that Jewish life had not always been that way. In fact, life for the Jewish people has rarely been as wonderful and comfortable and free over the course of the last two millennia. Rather, Jewish history has been a long and arduous journey that began in the Promised Land, and which continued through two exiles, to the *"four quarters of the earth"* (Isaiah 11:12), leaving a trail of persecution, destruction, and terror. On my mother's side, my family is descended from survivors of the Holocaust, the darkest chapter in history during which one-third of the world's Jewish population was systematically killed at the

hands of the Nazis. On my father's side, I come from ten generations who clung to the land of Israel, miraculously surviving wars
and famines, until they could no longer hold on and fled to the
U.S. in 1928. Both my parents grew up in a generation that assim-
ilated into the mainstream culture and abandoned their Jewish
identity at an alarming rate. In my own generation, more than half
of American Jews have left their faith and married outside of the
Jewish community.

When I look back on the history of my people, and even my
own family, I cannot help but wonder. How did we, as a people,
survive? How is it possible that we lived through such physical hard-
ship and yet maintained our spiritual connection when the odds
were against us? How did my parents maintain their faith when it
would have been so much easier to blend in with everyone else?
One answer, of course, is that the God of Abraham, Isaac, and Jacob,
has always protected and guarded the apple of His eye, Israel. The
other answer can be found in the steadfast commitment in Judaism
to pass down our faith to the next generation, what has come to be
known as *l'dor v'dor*, לדור ודור, from generation to generation.

———

This responsibility to pass on the faith from one generation to the
next is imbedded into the very DNA of the nation of Israel. On the
eve of the Exodus of the Israelites from Egypt, Moses had but one

recurring message for the people of Israel: Teach your children —
share your story, tell them about God's greatness, your faith, and
God's miracles. Moses entreated the people to teach the next generation no less than three times on that historic night. First, just
after he gave them God's instructions regarding the Passover lamb
sacrifice, Moses told the people, "*When you enter the land that the
LORD will give you ... And when your children ask you, 'What does
this ceremony mean to you?' then tell them, 'It is the Passover sacrifice
to the LORD, who passed over the houses of the Israelites in Egypt and
spared our homes ...*'" (Exodus 12:25–27). In the instructions Moses
gave the people for observing the Passover, he reminded them, "*On
that day tell your son, 'I do this because of what the LORD did for me
when I came out of Egypt*'" (Exodus 13:8). And again, just as the
Israelites were about to leave Egypt, Moses said, "*In days to come,
when your son asks you, 'What does this mean?' say to him, 'With
a mighty hand the LORD brought us out of Egypt, out of the land of
slavery*'" (Exodus 13:14). From the very beginning of the nation,
teaching the next generation and passing on the faith was presented
as a vital factor in the success and survival of Israel.

Similarly, as the nation of Israel stood on the banks of the
Jordan River, poised to finally enter the land promised to Abraham,
Isaac, and Jacob, God gave them the quintessential declaration of
faith and directed them to teach it to their children. Once again, at
a critical juncture in history, there was an emphasis on educating

the next generation. This Scripture, known as the *Shema* prayer, is recited every morning and evening by observant Jews. It states:

> *"Hear O Israel, the LORD our God, the LORD is one. Love the LORD your God with all your heart and with all your soul, and with all your strength. These commandments I give you today are to be on your hearts. Impress them on your children."* — DEUTERONOMY 6:4-7A.

Not only that, but Jewish mothers and fathers are commanded to talk about God's laws and His values with their children constantly, *"when you sit at home and when you walk along the road, when you lie down and when you get up"* (Deuteronomy 6:7b). Moreover, this obligation of passing on the faith and educating our children is intended to begin at their earliest age. As King Solomon taught, *"Start children off on the way they should go, and even when they are old they will not turn from it"* (Proverbs 22:6). To that end, Jewish parents recite the *Shema* with their children as they tuck them into bed at night long before their children can even speak.

There is a stirring story told about Rabbi Yitzhak HaLevi Herzog, a 20th-century Israeli rabbi, who was tasked with finding the many Jewish orphans left in Europe in the wake of the Holocaust during World War II. In 1946, he traveled to a large monastery that had taken in dozens of Jewish children in order to save them from the Nazis. Jewish parents had sent them in order to protect them, intending to reclaim their children after the war. Only, almost none of the parents survived.

When Rabbi Herzog arrived at the monastery, he thanked the Reverend Mother for saving the children and requested their return now that the war was over. The nun replied that she was happy to return the children to their rightful place, but explained that there was no way to tell which of the hundreds of children in the orphanage were Jewish. The children were too young when they came, and separated from their parents for too long since their arrival to remember anything about being Jewish. Rabbi Herzog replied that he would find a way.

"Having children is more than a gift. It's a responsibility."

Rabbi Herzog asked the Reverend Mother to gather all the children in the large hall at the orphanage. Once she did, he ascended the stage and cried in a loud voice, *"Shema Yisrael, Hashem Elokainu, Hashem echad!"* "Hear O Israel, the LORD our God, the LORD is one!" Immediately, dozens of children rushed toward the rabbi yelling, "Mama," "Papa," with tears in their eyes. Many of them sobbed uncontrollably. Their true identity was revealed by the words that their parents had, indeed, impressed upon them from the time that they were born.

This commitment to educating the next generation and passing on our faith has been key to the survival of the Jewish people throughout the ages. Rabbi Jonathan Sacks, the former chief rabbi of the United Kingdom, once wrote, "Having children is more than a gift. It's a responsibility. For us as Jews, it's the most sacred responsibility there is. On it depends the future of the Jewish people. For four thousand years our people survived because in every generation, Jews made it their highest priority to hand their faith on to their children."

I have witnessed this myself in my own family. In a letter that my *Saba* (grandfather), Rabbi Simon Eckstein, wrote to my father, he said:

> "You were reared in a rabbi's home, where, thank
> G-d, you were able to absorb Jewish traditional
> values about all aspects of life. In our frequent
> discussions, we always gave priority to the need
> to perform deeds of *chesed* — acts of charity,
> kindness, and thoughtfulness. Fondly, we
> remember how we sat around the dinner table
> on *Shabbat* and sang our favorite songs — songs
> that your mother and I learned from our parents.
> Even as children, your brother and sisters would
> help us as we distributed food to the needy
> during the High Holy Days and Passover."

My grandfather ended his note with these words, "As people grow older (especially at the grandparent stage), they feel blessed by G-d when they see that the heritage (*mesorah*) and their traditional values which the received from their own parents and grandparents are now being passed on to one's next generation."

The more we shine with the light of our own faith, the more we will spread the light of God — to our children, their children, and beyond.

While my father passed away far too early, I feel blessed to know that he was able to witness this chain of faith from his parents being passed on, not only to my sisters and me, but to his grand-children. The lessons he cherished most from his parents — respect for elders, compassion toward the most vulnerable in our society, and devoting time and energy toward helping others — he was so proud to see manifested in his grandchildren.

Ultimately, passing on the faith has remained, and is still primar-ily accomplished through the home and family life. The main way that Jewish mothers and fathers transmit Jewish values and ideas is through the biblically mandated holy days God commanded the

Israelites to observe. These observances and rituals have bonded Jewish families and communities and kept their faith alive through exiles, dispersions, inquisitions, pogroms, persecution, and yes, even the Holocaust.

Rabbi Ken Spiro writes, "Family life is regarded as a training ground for the Jewish way of life. Children receive their earliest education in the home. Parents show them how to live as Jews. Jewish parents are expected to make the home a place where Judaism is alive. They can do this through acts of Jewish worship, such as the weekly *Shabbat* celebration or marking the Jewish festivals." The wondrous thing about God's holy days and observances is that they have a way of communicating faith with children of every age and adults at every stage of life. They provide experiences rich with meaning and spirit that transcend the limits of language and traditional instruction. It is these gatherings and memories that plant the seeds of values such as faith, wisdom, hope, courage, forgiveness, gratitude, generosity, and setting priorities; it is repeating these traditions and rituals year after year that makes them flourish and grow.

Together, in the pages ahead, we will explore these Jewish holidays and observances, along with the key value instilled within them. My hope is that in sharing my experiences and the lessons that I have learned from my parents, these will inform and inspire you, and that these lessons will serve as tools to help you in passing your faith to your children. Ultimately, we are all called, Christians and Jews, to be living examples of faith for our children. In the Christian Bible, the apostle Paul taught, *"Fathers, do not exasperate your children; instead, bring them up in the training and instruction of the Lord"* (Ephesians 6:4). And in his instructions to his young protégé in faith, Timothy, Paul wrote, *"Don't let anyone look down on you because you are young, but set an example for the believers in speech, in conduct, in love, in faith and in purity"* (1 Timothy 4:12).

The more we shine with the light of our own faith, the more we will spread the light of God — to our children, their children, and beyond.

לְדוֹר וָדוֹר

L'DOR V'DOR

SHABBAT

TEACHING OUR CHILDREN PRIORITIES

"'It will be a sign between me and the Israelites
forever, for in six days the LORD made the heavens
and the earth, and on the seventh day he rested
and was refreshed.'" — EXODUS 31:17

"One can say without exaggeration
that more than Israel has kept
the Sabbath, the Sabbath has
kept and preserved Israel."

— *Ahad Ha'am, (1856–1927), Hebrew essayist and founder of
cultural Zionism*

OUR CHILDREN TODAY ARE GROWING UP IN THE MOST TECH-
nologically advanced generation the world has ever witnessed. Unlike previous generations, who also enjoyed more technology than their parents did, our world is changing much faster,
and the effects are far greater than before. Unsurprisingly, this has
had a profound impact on every aspect of our lives, including the
most important ones: family, friends, community, and our connection to God.

On the positive side, technology has given us the ability to "stay
connected" and communicate more often and more easily. We can
video chat, send messages, share photos, and speak to one another

from just about anywhere in the world with the simple press of a button. We can also receive and share ideas, inspiration, and knowledge via the internet that undoubtedly help us live better lives.

However, there also is an adverse side to technology. Children *and* adults are spending more time on electronic devices and less time together with family and friends. Moreover, as society has advanced technologically, life has become increasingly busy. Parents work longer hours, and children have busier after-school schedules than just a decade ago. Statistics show that the average American family spends only 35–50 minutes talking to each other on weekdays and less than three hours in meaningful engagement on weekends. Family meals are far less common than they used to be, although studies have proven that eating together as a family several days a week improves a child's health, grades, and emotional stability. Day after day, week after week, year after year, our lives rush by, but we still don't have significant time for what matters most.

In the Ten Commandments, the Fourth Commandment, sacred to both the Jewish and Christian faiths, directs us to observe a day of rest, the Sabbath. Jews observe the Sabbath from Friday at sundown until Saturday at sundown, while Christians observe it on Sunday. The Hebrew word for Sabbath is *Shabbat*, and while it is commonly translated as "rest," a more accurate translation is "stop." The Scriptures say, *"For six days work is to be done, but the seventh day is a day of (שבת, Shabbat) sabbath rest, holy to the LORD ... for in six days the*

LORD *made the heavens and the earth, and on the seventh day* (שבת, *Shabbat*) *he rested and was refreshed"* (Exodus 31:15–17).

We are directed to work for six days and then stop working on the seventh, just as God created the world in six days and then stopped creating on the seventh. *Shabbat* beckons us to pause, reflect, refresh, and redirect our lives in a way that is congruent with our values. The Hebrew word *Shabbat* is also closely related to the word *shav*, which means "return." The Sabbath is a day to return to our priorities.

The Sabbath reminds us that while we must work in life, life must never become about work.

In summer 2010, Israeli Prime Minister Benjamin Netanyahu was interviewed on Larry King Live. Larry King said to him, "You live in the center of a hostile world. Do you ever get to really relax?" Netanyahu answered, "Yes, and I'll tell you when. Every Saturday we have a day off (*Shabbat*). I take an hour and a half, and I read from the Bible with my younger boy. I relax then and I draw a lot of spiritual strength."

Shabbat has always been a source of strength and a conduit for clarity among the Jewish people. Beginning the Sabbath by lighting the *Shabbat* candles reflects this belief. The Jewish sages taught that gazing at these flames repairs our vision. In other words, all week long, we can lose perspective. Our vision can become distorted regarding our value and goals. However, the light of *Shabbat* reminds us of what really matters and invites us to focus exclusively on what is most important to us.

—

I grew up in a very loving family. We enjoyed an abundance of love, but like many families today, we were very busy. My father woke up at 5 a.m. for prayer and Bible study, and then left for work so that he could be at the office by 7 a.m. My mother started her day a bit later, but once she got us off to school, she went to work as well. My sisters and I had long days at a school that taught both secular subjects and Jewish studies. In addition, my parents dedicated their time and talents to volunteering in our community. My sisters and I participated in Jewish youth groups and after-school activities. Our lives were blessedly wonderful — and hectic. In a sea of busyness, *Shabbat* was — and is — the anchor of my life.

No matter how busy our weeks were or how much my father had traveled — no matter what — he made it a priority that on *Shabbat* we were all together as a family. My mother cooked our favorite foods, baked *challah* (the traditional Sabbath bread), and cleaned our home from top to bottom. As my sisters and I grew older, we loved to participate as well, getting many of our first cooking (and cleaning!) lessons as we helped prepare for the holy day of rest. My father often played music to set the mood — traditional Jewish songs related to the Sabbath. As sundown drew closer, the tempo in the house quickened as we finished our final preparations.

Then, just before sunset, everything stopped and quiet set in. The music was turned off, the cooking was done, the house was ready. I stood with my mother as she lit the *Shabbat* candles and recited the traditional blessing welcoming the Sabbath. We kissed each other and wished each other *Shabbat shalom*, a Sabbath of peace. My father left for synagogue, and I often went with him. We joined our community in soulful singing and worship. Friday night *Shabbat* prayers begin: "*Come, let us sing for joy to the LORD; let us shout aloud to the Rock of our salvation. Let us come before him with thanksgiving and extol him with music and song*" (Psalm 95:1–2). *Shabbat* gave me time each week to reflect on God's glory and His blessings.

I feel the need for a Sabbath day more than I ever did before.

After services, we returned home to a beautifully set table and a delicious meal. Unlike during the week, no one rushed anywhere. We talked about our week, laughed, sang, and discussed inspiring ideas from the *Torah*. I used to joke that our *Shabbat* meals were like holy therapy sessions, but that is truly what it felt like. *Shabbat* gave us permission to let go of our worries and fill our souls with godliness. Around the *Shabbat* table, we were unbound by the constraints of weekdays and had limitless time to focus on God and each other. Jewish sages taught that the Sabbath is "a taste of the world to come." Indeed, for us, it was — and is — a little taste of paradise.

———

Of the many contributions Judaism has made to humanity, *Shabbat* is perhaps the most important. Devoting one day a week for rest and contemplation is one of the greatest gifts that Judaism has brought to the world.

While the Sabbath has been universally acclaimed, it also, at times, has been grossly misunderstood. It is commonly believed that *Shabbat* is observed in order to replenish our physical strength and enable us to work more energetically and productively during the coming week. However, in Judaism, the exact opposite is true. While many people rest on the weekend in preparation for the workweek ahead, Judaism implores us to work during the week *in order to rest on Shabbat*. In the Jewish faith, the Sabbath is the endpoint, the goal, the culmination of the week.

This is why there are no Hebrew names for the first six days of the week. Instead, they are known by the number of days remaining until *Shabbat*. Sunday is called *yom rishon beshabbat*, or "the first day toward *Shabbat*," Monday is *yom shainee beshabbat*, or "the second day toward *Shabbat*," and so on. Every day is a countdown to the one day that matters most. Only the seventh day, the Sabbath, has a name: *Shabbat,* stop, rest.

The Sabbath reminds us that while we must work in life, life must never become about work. It serves as a weekly reminder that life is about connecting with God, our families, friends, communities, and ultimately, about making the world a better place. Moreover, the Sabbath recalls that God is the Creator and Master over the world, keeping our human role in proper perspective. It is, as Rabbi Abraham Joshua Heschel once called it, "an island in time," where we can collectively recalibrate our focus on what really matters.

For one day in seven, we live on this "island in time," where time itself is suspended and we cease to be enslaved by it. The Sabbath is a day of spiritual connection in the context of physical rest. It's a day to recognize God as the Master of the universe and to study His Word. We don't refrain from working just so that we can have a short break before we go back to the grind the next day; we rest from activity so that we can exercise our soul.

In the words of Heschel, the purpose of *Shabbat* is, "To set apart one day a week for freedom, a day on which we would not use the instruments which have been so easily turned into weapons of destruction, a day for being with ourselves, a day of detachment from the vulgar, of independence of external obligations, a day on which we stop worshiping the idols of technical civilization, a day on which we use no money, a day of armistice in the economic struggle with our fellow men and the forces of nature ..."

Heschel concludes, "Is there any institution that holds out a greater hope for man's progress than the Sabbath?"

In this day and age, with the constant barrage of information and motion, the *Shabbat* experience is more important than ever. In our fast-paced society, where it's easy to lose oneself in the hustle and bustle of it all, *Shabbat* is essential for slowing down, finding one's self, and hearing the still small voice of God. On *Shabbat*, we are able to press the pause button on the busy schedule of life and take time to focus on what really matters. No one checks email, answers a phone, or gets in a car to go anywhere. We are simply present — with each other and with God.

Perhaps there is no generation more in need of *Shabbat* than our own.

For me, *Shabbat* is a welcome respite from my hectic schedule in my many roles as a mother, wife, and president and CEO of a major nonprofit organization. I thank God that *Shabbat* arrives every seventh day. It is usually around then that our family needs a break and a reminder that life is not about being busy. As a mother, I feel the need for a Sabbath day more than I ever did before. It is the one day a week that we "unplug," so that we can connect with each other.

In our home, we begin preparing for *Shabbat* on Thursday night. Everything that we do is a physical reminder of what is spiritually important to us as a family. My children love making the special *Shabbat* bread, *challah,* with me, and I embrace the change of pace as we wind down together. Just as my father did, we play *Shabbat*-themed music which helps us transition from feeling stressed to feeling blessed. As the heavenly smell of freshly baked *challah* fills our home, we anticipate the holy day of *Shabbat*.

By the time Friday evening arrives, our *Shabbat* table is beautifully set, my children are dressed in their nicest clothing, and the *Shabbat* candlesticks are polished and shiny. Little details, like a special tablecloth, flowers on the table, and favorite foods on the menu reinforce the message that *Shabbat* is the most special day of the week. My children understand that the things that we do on *Shabbat* — like making time for God, family, and friends — are clearly the priorities in our lives.

As the sun sets on Friday, my daughters join me as we light the Sabbath candles to usher in this sacred time. Traditionally, we light a candle for every member of our family. Jewish tradition teaches that candle-lighting time is an ideal time for prayer, and so the first thing my children see me do as the Sabbath enters is pray for them. We wrap our arms around each other as we sing and pray.

My husband usually arrives home from synagogue with a few guests. We enjoy having guests at our *Shabbat* table, so my children learn that welcoming people into our home and sharing a meal with them is another family priority. Sometimes, we have friends or family over, but often, we'll host people that we barely know, such as a lonely widow, a lone soldier, or a new immigrant to Israel. During the week, we have so much to do that we often overlook these very people who are in need all around us. We don't have time for them. But on *Shabbat*, we have all the time in the world, and we eagerly turn our attention to God and all His children.

Before we sit down to eat our delicious meal, we bless our children. It is Jewish tradition to bestow the priestly blessing onto our children on *Shabbat*. We lay our hands over each child's head, starting with the oldest, and bless them. In this way, each child feels noticed, cared for, and loved. Next, like most Jewish families, we sing the words of Proverbs 31 in praise of the woman of the home. It's a teachable moment for our children when we take the time to acknowledge and appreciate the hard work that goes into maintaining a home. Finally we bless the *Shabbat* over a cup of wine and begin the meal with *challah*.

These Friday night dinners are our time to ask each child about his or her week. We celebrate the highlights and sympathize with the challenges. It's a time to discuss the portion from the *Torah* that is read that week, and what they have learned in school from the Scriptures. In between courses, we sing Sabbath songs, some of which are hundreds of years old. There are no time limits to our *Shabbat* meals. No one is rushing through the meal to get to another activity or to watch a TV program. We are all fully present with those at our table.

On Saturday, we join our community in the synagogue for prayers. Not only does this teach our children that prayer is a top priority, but also that being part of a faith community is important as well. After services, there is often a light meal served in order to foster fellowship within the community.

As the day unfolds, we enjoy the second *Shabbat* meal together with joy, love, and holiness, just as we did on Friday night. If our children want to get together with their friends after the meal, they have to walk to their houses or make plans before *Shabbat* — talking on the phone or over social media is not an option. Neither is watching a movie or playing video games. My children are most creative with their friends on Saturday afternoons when they come up with endless ways to entertain themselves. Sometimes they play imaginary games, other times they play board games, and the older kids sit and talk. It is a slow-paced, people-focused, and God-honoring time.

I do not know what kind of world my children will live in when they are adults. Maybe it will be even more saturated with the latest technological distractions and even faster-paced. However, what I do know is that no matter what life has in store for them, my children will always have *Shabbat*. They will always have that refuge, that "island of time," to rest, to stop, to recalibrate and refocus on what is truly important so that they can live meaningful, purposeful, godly lives.

SABBATH IN THE NEW TESTAMENT

On numerous occasions in the New Testament, we find Jesus at odds with the religious leaders of the time over the keeping — or breaking — of the Sabbath rest. And when he rebuked them, saying *"The Sabbath was made for man, not man for the Sabbath"* (Mark 2:27), Jesus was echoing the intent of the Sabbath as a day of rest, as stated in the Ten Commandments and elsewhere (See Deuteronomy 5:14; Isaiah 58:13–14). In fact, we read throughout the New Testament of Jesus observing the Sabbath by going to synagogue *"as was his custom"* and teaching (Luke 4:16). Certainly, Paul and his followers observed the Sabbath as well (Acts 16:13; 17:2; 18:4). The author of Hebrews wrote, *"There remains, then, a Sabbath-rest for the people of God; for anyone who enters God's rest also rests from their works, just as God did from his"* (Hebrews 4:9–10).

FAMILY TIME — TEACHING OUR CHILDREN TO SET PRIORITIES

1. Make a list of the top three things that are most important to each family member. Share what is on your list with each other. How does knowing God and obeying Him fit into your priorities?

2. Read the story of Mary and Martha in Luke 10:38–42 together. What did each sister consider the most important thing to do in serving Jesus? What did Jesus say was most important? How can we demonstrate that God is most important to us?

3. Dr. Jim Burns, Ph.D., a Christian author and renowned youth and family expert, wrote, "The key is not to prioritize what's on your schedule, but to schedule your priorities." What does that look like for your family? Spend time to identify your family's priorities and then work to schedule them into your week.

For Parents

Yael wrote, "My children will always have *Shabbat*. They will always have that refuge, that 'island of time,' to rest, to stop, to recalibrate and refocus on what is truly important so that they can live meaningful, purposeful, godly lives." How can you help your children refocus each week on what is meaningful and purposeful?

Memory Verses

Select one of the verses below for you and your family to memorize
and use as a guide on setting priorities.

> *Love the LORD your God with all your heart*
> *and with all your soul and with all your*
> *strength.* — DEUTERONOMY 6:5

> *"Be still, and know that I am God."* — PSALM 46:10

> *Seek the LORD while he may be found;*
> *call on him while he is near.* — ISAIAH 55:6

> *"But seek first his kingdom and his righteousness,*
> *and all these things will be given to you*
> *as well."* — MATTHEW 6:33

> *Do not conform to the pattern of this world, but be*
> *transformed by the renewing of your mind. Then you*
> *will be able to test and approve what God's will is — his*
> *good, pleasing and perfect will.* — ROMANS 12:2

לְדוֹר וָדוֹר

L'DOR V'DOR

PASSOVER

TEACHING OUR CHILDREN TO SEEK KNOWLEDGE

indeed, if you call out for insight
   and cry aloud for understanding,
and if you look for it as for silver
   and search for it as for hidden treasure,
then you will understand the fear of the LORD
   and find the knowledge of God. — PROVERBS 2:3-5

"We are closer to God when we
are asking questions than when
we think we have the answers."

— *Rabbi Abraham Joshua Heschel, (1907–1972), Polish-American
rabbi and leading Jewish theologian of the 20th century*

JUDAISM IS A RELIGION OF QUESTIONS. ON ONE HAND, WE ARE
called to believe God's promises and trust His providence. On
the other, we have a tradition of questioning God's ways, asking the
weighty questions in life, and seeking the answers. Asking questions
is not at odds with faith; rather, it is the means by which we deepen
our faith and express our desire to know God. This is why Rabbi
Abraham Joshua Heschel contended that asking questions brings
us closer to God; indeed, it is part of our divine service and duty.

The first Jewish patriarch, Abraham, had questions. When
God informed him that He intended to destroy the entire city
of Sodom, Abraham replied, "*Will not the Judge of all the earth
do right?*" (Genesis 18:25). Moses questioned God, as well. When

Pharaoh increased the labor of the Israelites in response to Moses' demands, Moses asked God, "*Why, Lord, why have you brought trouble on this people?*" (Exodus 5:22).

The prophet Jeremiah did not hold back his questions, either. He asked God possibly one of the most pressing questions for all people of faith through the ages:

> *You are always righteous, LORD,*
> > *when I bring a case before you.*
> *Yet I would speak with you about your justice:*
> > *Why does the way of the wicked prosper?*
> > *Why do all the faithless live at ease?* — JEREMIAH 12:1

Clearly, we see from this exchange that Jeremiah was completely comfortable in bringing his questions before God, no matter how difficult the subject.

Perhaps most famously, the book of Job is filled with man's questions for God, and God's answers are filled with more questions for man. And in the Christian Bible, one of the earliest records of Jesus is as a 12-year-old boy, in the Temple, asking questions of the rabbis: "*After three days they found him* [Jesus] *in the temple courts, sitting among the teachers, listening to them and asking them questions*" (Luke 2:46).

The *Talmud*, Judaism's Oral Tradition later recorded in written form, is presented in a question-and-answer format. A topic is typically introduced with a question and responded to with more questions until a viable answer is found. If you enter a Jewish *Torah* study hall today, you will not encounter the prevailing silence of a college lecture hall. Instead, you will witness students in passionate discussion, even shouting at one another, as study partners challenge each other as a way of discerning the truth.

The Jewish fascination with questioning comes down to this: In order to serve God and become the best version of ourselves, we must constantly seek to learn and grow — and in order to learn, one must ask questions.

Dr. Isidor Rabi, Jewish physicist and recipient of the 1944 Nobel Prize for Physics, was once asked why he became a scientist. He replied, "My mother made me a scientist without ever intending it. Every other mother in Brooklyn would ask her child after school: 'So? Did you learn anything today?' But not my mother. She always asked me a different question. 'Izzy,' she would say, 'did you ask a good question today?' That difference — asking good questions — made me become a scientist!"

Jews have long been known as "The People of the Book" — the people through whom the world received the Bible, and the people who have incessantly studied God's Word for thousands of years. As a natural corollary, Jews have become known as a people who value the study of all things, regarding the seeking of knowledge as a supreme value.

We see this repeatedly throughout both the Jewish and Christian Bible. When God asked Solomon what it was he most wanted, Solomon asked for wisdom: "*give your servant a discerning heart to govern your people and to distinguish between right and wrong. For who is able to govern this great people of yours?*" (1 Kings 3:9). And in the Christian Bible, the apostle James advised, "*If any of you lacks wisdom, you should ask God, who gives generously to all without finding fault, and it will be given to you*" (James 1:5).

During the holiday of Passover, we harness the power of questions in order to teach the next generation about our history, our values, and God's promise for our future.

However, what most people do not know is that the secret to wisdom and learning is asking questions. The rabbis taught that a person who has no questions has no space to receive new knowledge. He is literally full of himself. However, one who asks questions creates space for answers, new ideas, and possibilities that can enter one's mind and settle into one's soul.

The Hebrew word for wisdom is *chochma*, חכמה, and by switching the first two letters, the word reads *coach ma*, כח מה, which literally means, "the power of 'what?'" In other words, wisdom is gained through the power of asking questions.

It is quite fitting then that Jews commemorate the most important event in our history, the Exodus from Egypt, by asking questions. During the holiday of Passover, we harness the power of questions in order to teach the next generation about our history, our values, and God's promise for our future.

~

One of my first childhood memories is at our family *seder*, the ritual Passover meal. I am the youngest of three daughters, and so once I was old enough to read, it was my job to ask the traditional "Four Questions" at the outset of the *seder*. I can remember standing on a chair in my nice new dress while the entire family looked at me in proud expectation. After I recited the four questions in Hebrew, everyone cheered, and the *seder* began.

At the time, I didn't understand that what I was doing had been performed by the youngest child for thousands upon thousands of years. I was simply the next in a long line of ancestors to ask these questions on Passover eve. I also did not understand the importance or significance of asking questions. However, it was clear to me — and to every child who has recited these four questions — that asking was a good thing.

In later years, a younger cousin would assume the role of asking "The Four Questions," and my attention turned to questions of my own. One of my most vivid memories is my father eating an entire tablespoon of traditional bitter herbs, in this case, horse-radish. It was so bitter that my father's eyes filled with tears, and it looked as though he was weeping at our holiday meal.

I asked my father why he was crying, and he responded, "So that you would ask!" One of my older sisters then explained that the purpose of eating bitter herbs was to remind us of the bitter enslavement of the Israelites and the tears that they shed. From my father's perspective, he was just as proud of me for asking the question as he was with my sister for knowing the answer.

Another year, I watched my father help my mother meticulously clean our refrigerator in preparation for Passover. They scrubbed and cleaned every single part and got rid of food that I now know was *chametz* (leavened food products). I could not understand why they were doing that or what it had to do with Passover or the Exodus so I asked my father. He beamed at me with his big broad smile and replied, "I'm so glad that you asked! This is the beginning of what Passover is all about. It's all about asking questions."

Passover is one of the most celebrated and widely observed holidays for Jewish people around the world. It is at the heart of the nation of Israel, bringing together family and friends of multiple generations and diverse backgrounds to commemorate the seminal event in Jewish history, the Exodus. At the core of Passover is the *seder*, the ritual meal held on the first night. The focus of the *seder* is retelling the Exodus narrative and hearing the story as if for the first time. This annual storytelling energizes the Jewish people and is one of the forces that has held them together for millennia — through exiles, pogroms, persecution, and yes, even the Holocaust.

In fact, on the eve of the very first Passover, God commanded Israel to observe the holiday on the very same day every year, *"This is a day you are to commemorate; for the generations to come you shall celebrate it as a festival to the LORD—a lasting ordinance* (Exodus 12:14).

… our children are the most important guests at the table, and the *seder* revolves around them.

During Temple times, Jews brought a Passover lamb offering as prescribed by God in Exodus 12:3–4 and shared it with their families along with bitter herbs and *matzah* (Exodus 12:8). Today, as the Temple no longer stands, the focus of the holiday is the *seder*, through which we fulfill the biblical injunction to *"tell your children and grandchildren how I dealt harshly with the Egyptians and how I performed my signs among them"* (Exodus 10:2).

Seder literally means "order," and the Passover *seder* is a deliberately designed experience containing 15 steps placed in a specific order. The main part of the *seder* is the fifth step, the *maggid*, which means "telling," as in telling the story. This is the heart of the *seder* and the essence of Passover. It is here that we tell the story of the Exodus through biblical scriptures, songs, rituals, and commentary.

Yet, when we tell the story of the Exodus, we do not begin with a description of events. Instead, at every *seder,* the story begins not with answers and explanations, but with questions. In many communities, the leader dresses up as an Israelite slave leaving Egypt, and the guests ask, "Where are you coming from?" The leader replies, "I am coming from Egypt." The guests continue, "And where are you going?" The leader responds, "I am going to Jerusalem." This question-answer format, along with visual aids and audience participation, is intended to capture the imagination of children and sets the tone for the evening.

Indeed, our children are the most important guests at the table, and the *seder* revolves around them. "The Four Questions," one of the most iconic and memorable Passover passages, is traditionally sung at the *seder* by the youngest child able to do so. Incidentally, if no children are present then one of the adults must recite the questions. Moreover, if a person is alone, he or she must ask themselves "The Four Questions." Such is the value that Judaism places on asking before receiving answers.

"The Four Questions" highlight four unusual aspects of the *seder* that were instituted by the Jewish sages for the sole purpose of piquing a child's curiosity. The text begins, "Why is this night different from all other nights?" and specifies four questions:

On all other nights, we eat leavened bread and
unleavened bread. Why do we only eat *matzah*
(unleavened bread) on this night?

On all other nights, we eat all kinds of vegetables.
Why do we eat only bitter herbs on this night?

On all other nights, we need not dip our vegetables at
all. Why do we dip vegetables twice on this night?

On all other nights, we can eat leaning or sitting up
straight. Why on this night do we only eat reclining?

The reason that we begin our story with questions is because
of the verse that says: "*In days to come, when your son asks you,
'What does this mean?' say to him, 'With a mighty hand the* LORD
brought us out of Egypt ...'" (Exodus 13:14). The Bible specifies that
our children should ask first, and then we should answer. "The Four
Questions" also provide the springboard to discuss with our children the fundamental ideas of the Jewish faith found in the Exodus
story — that God is with us in our suffering, that He hears our
prayers, that He cares about His people, and that He intervenes in
human history to bring about salvation.

As the old saying goes, "Tell me and I forget, teach me and
I remember, involve me and I learn." The *seder* was intelligently

designed to involve children to the greatest extent, mostly by way of eliciting questions, but also through other hands-on experiences.

While the *seder* is a powerful educational tool that we revisit every Passover, the overall objective is to encourage our children to ask questions all year long. "To be a Jewish child is to learn how to question," explains Rabbi Jonathan Sacks, who served as Chief Rabbi of Britain from 1991 to 2013. "Against cultures that see unquestioning obedience as the ideal behavior of a child, Jewish tradition, in the *Haggadah* (the written guide to the *seder*), regards the 'child who has not learned to ask' as the lowest, not the highest, stage of development."

Judaism maintains that true faith can only come through asking questions, seeking answers, and choosing God as an act of freedom rather than an imposed state of being. Our goal is to ensure that our children will be seekers of God and the wisdom of the Bible for the rest of their lives.

Throughout our children's school years, the typical educational model tends to be memorizing information and repeating it on tests. Even as our schools progress and incorporate new learning techniques, the very fact that there are more than 10 students in a class means that educators have to do more talking and children get to do less asking if they are to cover the required amount of material.

It is therefore the job of parents to encourage children to ask questions and seek knowledge. There is no substitute for a child's natural curiosity when it comes to learning, and we must nurture it. Albert Einstein once said: "I have no special talent. I am only passionately curious." Imagine a world full of passionately curious adults like Einstein — God only knows what ideas would be uncovered and how many problems would be solved.

Passover gives my husband and me the opportunity to light the fire of curiosity in the souls of our children. We praise our children at the *seder* when they ask questions. The answers that we provide — how God saved His people through ten miraculous plagues and the parting of the sea — spark even more curiosity and imagination. When it is age-appropriate, we will often answer our children's questions with more questions that guide them toward finding answers on their own. Moreover, there is no age limit to learning something new, and the adults at the *seder* ask questions of their own, modeling for our children the value of learning that never ends.

Like many Jewish children, the moment from Passover that my children remember most is when it is their turn to ask "The Four Questions." Typically, children are four or five years old when they are ready to ask the questions, often in front of 10, 20, or 50 other people. After the text is recited — successfully or not — we cheer for the children, giving them the unmistakable impression that asking questions is a very good thing.

Our Jewish tradition teaches, "A person who is shy cannot learn." A person who is too shy to ask a question will miss countless learning opportunities. The first experience that our children have with asking questions is an overwhelmingly affirmative one, creating a positive association with asking questions in the future.

As parents, we are all familiar with the stage that most children go through when all they ask is "why?" Why does the grass grow? Why do we have to brush our teeth? Why do we have to go to bed at 8 p.m.? Why does the sun go down every night? It's a seemingly endless stream of "whys," from the time they get up to the time they go to sleep. Too often, we are in a rush or have had enough of answering questions for the day, and is tempting to become irritated and shout back, "because that's just the way it is!"

As a mother, I try my best to answer my children's questions.

Yet, every Passover, I am reminded to treat these questions as holy. These seemingly inconsequential questions have a value beyond what I understand. Each time a child asks a question, it is an opportunity for us to encourage asking questions in the future, and consequently, to inspire a lifetime of learning.

There is another set of "four" in the Passover *seder* which is read about in the *Haggadah* shortly after "The Four Questions" are asked by the children. The text speaks about four children — the wise child, the rebellious child, the simple child, and the child who does not know how to ask questions. The first three children ask questions about Passover reflective of their personality, and the *Haggadah* provides answers taken from the Bible that are appropriate for each type of child.

When it comes to the child who doesn't know how to ask, instead of instructing the parent "you shall say to him ..." as with the first three children, the *Haggadah* reads, "You shall open the way for him ..." The parent is obligated in the Jewish tradition to help that child open up and ask the questions that are deep within. Indeed, not only are we required to answer our children's questions appropriately, we also must inspire them to ask even more questions.

As a mother, I try my best to answer my children's questions. I either give them the answer, tell them that we can discuss it later, or tell them that the question is a good one, but I do not know the answer yet. The important thing is not really the answer; it's the fact that they asked a question and expressed their curiosity in the first place.

Passover encourages children to ask questions and at the same time reminds parents that questioning is a sacred experience — one that we must take seriously and respond to accordingly. And by putting our children at the very center of the Passover celebration, we are reminded once again that our children are our future. The beginnings of a better tomorrow lie in the questions that our children ask today.

PASSOVER IN THE NEW TESTAMENT

Certainly, Jesus was more than a passing participant in the Passover celebration. Even as a young boy, we know that Jesus celebrated Passover with his family in Jerusalem as God had commanded (Luke 2:41–42). In fact, what Christians know as the Lord's Supper (or the Last Supper) was the Passover celebration. Matthew records the following, *"On the first day of the Festival of Unleavened Bread, the disciples came to Jesus and asked, "Where do you want us to make preparations for you to eat the Passover?" He replied, "Go into the city to a certain man and tell him, 'The Teacher says: My appointed time is near. I am going to celebrate the Passover with my disciples at your house.' So the disciples did as Jesus directed them and prepared the Passover"* (26:17–19). This same event is recorded in all four Gospels. Later, Paul in his letter to the church at Corinth referred to Jesus as *"our Passover lamb"* (1 Corinthians 5:7).

FAMILY TIME — TEACHING OUR CHILDREN TO SEEK KNOWLEDGE

1. Read the story of Jesus as a young boy going to the Temple courts in Luke 2:41–48. What does this tell you about the value of seeking knowledge and asking questions?

2. One of the practices in Judaism that Yael mentioned is to answer a question with another question. Read Mark 11:28–30 to see how Jesus did this. Then think of a question you can ask your family and tell them they can only respond by asking another question. See where this leads you!

3. Peter Abelard, a 12th-century French philosopher and theologian, once said, "The key to wisdom is this — constant and frequent questioning, for by doubting we are led to question, by questioning we arrive at the truth." As a family, discuss where you have found that to be true.

For Parents

Yael wrote, "The [Passover] *seder* is a powerful educational tool that we revisit every Passover ... to encourage our children to ask questions all year long." Consider what you can do to encourage your children to ask questions.

Memory Verses

Select one of the verses below for you and your family to memorize on the value of wisdom.

Choose my instruction instead of silver,
knowledge rather than choice gold. — PROVERBS 8:10

The heart of the discerning acquires knowledge,
for the ears of the wise seek it out. — PROVERBS 18:15

Apply your heart to instruction and
your ears to words of knowledge. — PROVERBS 23:12

And this is my prayer: that your love may abound
more and more in knowledge and depth of
insight, so that you may be able to discern what
is best and may be pure and blameless for the
day of Christ — PHILIPPIANS 1:9-10

If any of you lacks wisdom, you should ask God,
who gives generously to all without finding fault,
and it will be given to you. — JAMES 1:5

לְדוֹר וָדוֹר

L'DOR V'DOR

SHAVUOT

Teaching Our Children Gratitude

I will give thanks to you, Lord, with all my heart;
    I will tell of all your wonderful deeds.
I will be glad and rejoice in you;
    I will sing the praises of your name, O Most High.

    — PSALM 9:1-2

"It is gratefulness which makes the soul great."

— Rabbi Abraham Joshua Heschel, (1907–1972), Polish-American rabbi and leading Jewish theologian of the 20th century

IT HAS BEEN SAID THAT WHILE PREVIOUS GENERATIONS STRUG- gled to raise children with little or nothing, our generation's challenge is to raise children who have everything. Chances are that someone in a previous generation of our family once struggled to put food on the table, buy their children good shoes, and pay for education — basics that most of our children take for granted today. Less than a century ago, indoor plumbing was a luxury, clean running water was not a given, and computers were unheard of. The reality is that the way we live today is more luxurious than how kings lived for thousands of years. Whether we realize it or not — and whether our children know it or not — we live today with extraordinary abundance.

And yet, so many of us, both adults and children, feel that we do not have enough. This is because of another phenomenon of our times — incessant advertising and consumerism. We are bombarded by ads through all types of media designed to keep us focused on what we don't have and make us want things that we didn't even know we lacked. These ads create the illusion that "everyone else has it" so we should too. They promote an attitude of entitlement, which combined with our natural tendency to be jealous of what others have, creates an environment where it is extremely challenging to be satisfied and grateful for what we do have. These feelings of lack, entitlement, and jealousy create a tsunami of negativity that wipes away any joy we might have experienced living with the abundance that we do have. The result is that instead of feeling gratitude for the boundless blessings that God showers upon us every day, most people feel like they never have enough.

The irony is that although we live in extraordinarily abundant times, people feel less satisfied than ever. Is it surprising that the 2018 World Happiness Report ranked the United States as only the 19th happiest country even though the U.S. has one of the strongest economies in the world? Mind you, Israel — a country that struggles with terrorism, wars, lower working wages, and higher expenses — came in at 13, six notches higher than America. The 18th-century Hasidic teacher Rebbe Nachman of Breslov wrote, "Gratitude rejoices with her sister joy and is always ready to light a candle and have a party. Gratitude doesn't much like the old cronies of boredom, despair and taking life for granted." Indeed, gratitude and joy go hand in hand. Or as contemporary author Melodie Beattie wrote, "Gratitude unlocks the fullness of life. It turns what we have into enough, and more." As people of faith, we know that gratitude is an especially important value to pass down to our children. It is the foundation of their relationship with God and the key to their happiness.

One of my father's teachings that has remained with me throughout my life is that the very essence of being a Jew is, by definition, to be thankful. The word "Jew" is short for Judah, one of the twelve tribes of Israel and the tribe from which most Jewish people today are descended. When Leah gave birth to Judah, her fourth son, she chose a name that reflected her gratitude to God and named him Yehuda, declaring "*This time I will praise* [odeh] *the* LORD" (Genesis 29:35). The name Judah comes from the Hebrew word *hoda'a,* which literally means "thankfulness." My father taught me that gratitude is an essential part of my identity as a Jew and of my service to God.

The first Jewish prayer I was taught as a child was the *Modeh Ani.* The words begin, "*Modeh ani*" or "I am thankful … before you living King for mercifully returning my soul to me (for another day), great is your faithfulness." This prayer is to be said first thing every morning, upon awakening. From a very young age, I was taught to start my day with gratitude and gratefulness to God for the gift of life itself.

My parents reinforced a grateful attitude in other ways as well. I was taught to say please and thank you with an emphasis on the latter. Whenever I received a gift from my grandparents, relatives, or friends, my parents were not the ones to say, "Thank you." Instead, I was instructed to write a thank-you note myself. I remember being in second grade at the time and protesting that I did not even know how to spell well enough to write a note! My parents insisted that even a misspelled thank-you note straight from my heart was more meaningful then a short "thank you" over the telephone. Soon, it became a habit. Whenever I received a gift, I wrote a note.

... there is nothing that we could ever give to God that would fully express our gratitude for everything that He has given to us.

That small act that my parents insisted upon had a huge impact on me. I continued to write notes of gratefulness throughout my teenage years and beyond. I wrote thank-you notes for a variety of reasons, not only for gifts. After my father died, I found many thank-you notes that I had written to him that I had long forgotten about, but evidently, my father never did. They meant so much to him that he had kept them with him for all those years. I was deeply moved by finding those notes, and it occurred to me that if my father cherished my gratitude toward him so much, how much more does God, the Father of us all, appreciate our expressions of thankfulness? While it is hard to find the right words to adequately express our gratitude to God, I have always remembered the lesson from my childhood. An imperfectly written letter straight from my heart is more meaningful than the most eloquent Hallmark card. So, too, a prayer of gratitude straight from the heart, no matter how lacking it may be, is accepted by God and is beloved to Him.

Bringing to God the firstfruits — meaning the best of the harvest — is a tangible expression of our thankfulness and gratitude.

Certainly, God does not need anything from us. Undoubtedly, there is nothing that we could ever give to God that would fully express our gratitude for everything that He has given to us. However, God is not concerned with our physical gifts to Him. He loves the sentiments of gratitude behind those gifts. It does not matter how little or how much we have to offer, rather it is the recognition of the goodness that God has provided that makes the gifts meaningful. In the Christian Bible, Paul also taught that our heart is the key in bringing God our gifts, *"For if the willingness is there, the gift is acceptable according to what one has, not according to what one does not have"* (2 Corinthians 8:12).

———

In the Jewish faith, the principle of gratitude is intricately woven into the holy day known as *Shavuot,* one of the three pilgrimage festivals mandated in the Bible. In Leviticus 23, the Bible instructs us to observe the holiday of *Shavuot* seven weeks after Passover. *Shavuot,* appropriately, means "weeks," as it marks the conclusion of counting these specified weeks. (In old Greek and Latin, this same festival became known as Pentecost. Pentecost means "fifty," and like *Shavuot,* refers to the fifty days between Passover and the following holiday). On this holiday, also called the "Festival of Harvest," we are directed to, *"Celebrate the Festival of Harvest with the firstfruits of the crops you sow in your field"* (Exodus 23:16). The Hebrew word for "firstfruits" is *bikurim,* which gives the holiday its third biblical name, *Yom HaBikurim,* the *"day of firstfruits"* (Numbers 28:26). Bringing to God the firstfruits — meaning the best of the harvest — is a tangible expression of our thankfulness and gratitude.

Judaism's Oral Tradition provides a beautiful description of what bringing the firstfruits looked like in Temple times. When an Israelite saw the first emergence of one of the seven species of the land — wheat, barley, grapes, figs, pomegranate, olives, or dates, as designated in Deuteronomy 8:8 — he tied a string around it, designating it as his firstfruits. On *Shavuot*, these firstfruits were presented to God at the Holy Temple in Jerusalem (or before Temple times, at the Tabernacle). With great pomp and pageantry, the people traveled to Jerusalem with their firstfruits in a basket on their shoulders along with an ox adorned with gilded horns and a crown of olive tree branches to lead the way. Festive music and singing accompanied the joyful procession. When the pilgrims bearing fruit entered the city of Jerusalem, the city's artisans, officers, and governors greeted them saying, "Our people [of such and such a place], enter in peace!" Once at the Temple, the firstfruits were given to the priests, and the pilgrim recited a prescribed biblical passage from Deuteronomy 26:5–10, remembering the past difficulties that the nation of Israel encountered from the time of the Patriarch Jacob until they settled in the Promised Land, "*a land flowing with milk and honey*" (Deuteronomy 26:9). The ceremony concluded with giving thanks to God for the land and the fruit of the land and rejoicing in God's goodness: "*Then you and the Levites and the foreigners residing among you shall rejoice in all the good things the LORD your God has given to you and your household*" (Deuteronomy 26:11).

Since the destruction of the Second Temple in 70 CE, Jews were no longer able to observe this ritual, and *Shavuot* took on a different significance. Today, *Shavuot* is observed primarily as the day upon which Israel received the *Torah* on Mount Sinai 3,000 years ago. According to tradition, God gave the Ten Commandments to Israel on the 6th day of the Hebrew month *Sivan,* the same day as *Shavuot.* Accordingly, the focus of *Shavuot* today is on Bible study, including the widely held custom to stay up all night studying the Bible. It is true that we can no longer give God our firstfruits literally, but through all-encompassing Bible study, we *can* give God the best we have to offer Him spiritually as a sacrifice of thanksgiving. We give ourselves to God by studying His Word, dedicating our lives to His purposes, and by recognizing that He alone is the source of all blessings. In fact, in several places in the Scriptures, people of faith are referred to as "firstfruits," chosen by God for His holy purposes (Jeremiah 2:3; James 1:18; Revelation 14:4).

Shavuot and Passover are not only connected by virtue of the seven weeks between them, but the two holidays are also connected spiritually. The lesson of Passover is about our most difficult times and receiving God's help in order to pass through them. *Shavuot* is about the fruitful times in our lives, when everything is going well, and remembering that God is the source of all our blessings. On Passover, we remember that God is with us in our hard times. On *Shavuot,* we make sure that we do not forget God in our easier, bountiful seasons.

When life is difficult, it is natural to call out to God for help. When life gets comfortable, our tendency is to take things for granted. Scripture warns us repeatedly about this vulnerability. In Deuteronomy 8, God warns that *"when you eat and are satisfied, when you build fine houses and settle down, and when your herds and flocks grow large and your silver and gold increase and all you have is multiplied, then your heart will become proud and you will forget the LORD your God, who brought you out of Egypt, out of the land of slavery … You may say to yourself, 'My power and the strength of my hands have produced this wealth for me.' But remember the LORD your God, for it is he who gives you the ability to produce wealth …"* (vv.12–18).

The antidote to taking God's blessings for granted or attributing them to our own abilities is gratitude —to recognize God's gifts and thank Him for them. Scripture instructs us, *"When you have eaten and are satisfied, praise the LORD your God for the good land he has given you"* (Deuteronomy 8:10). Saying "thank you" to God sounds simple and easy; however, it is something that easily gets lost in the busyness of life. The practice of giving our first and best to God ensures we acknowledge that it all belongs to Him and that He is the source of all of our blessings. In a broader sense, giving God our firstfruits implies that we give to God's purposes with the best that we have and that we acknowledge His gifts with gratitude, praise, and celebration. As Maimonides, the renowned 12th-century rabbi and scholar wrote, "Everything that is for the sake of God should be of the best and most beautiful. When one builds a house of prayer, it should be more beautiful than his own dwelling. When one feeds the hungry, he should feed him of the best and sweetest of his table. Whenever one designates something of a holy purpose, he should sanctify the finest of his possession." When we do that, when we give to God in a way that gives *Him* the most glory, we are, in essence, giving God our complete and boundless gratitude for what we have.

Thankfulness begins with awareness — awareness of what we have, of what God has done for us, and of what He continues to do for us each and every day.

Moreover, the biblical prescription for offering firstfruits teaches us that full gratitude comes with appreciating the context of our blessings. Interestingly, the text that was read upon presenting the firstfruits from Deuteronomy begins all the way back with the Patriarch Jacob, his struggles, and his descent to Egypt: "*My father was a wandering Aramean, and he went down into Egypt ...*" (26:5). The narrative continues with the story of the Israelites, through their slavery in Egypt, to God bringing them out of Egypt to the land of milk and honey. The text concludes, "*... now I bring the firstfruits of the soil that you, LORD, have given me*" (26:10). Scripture goes through the entire story of Israel's difficulties, God's salvation, and God's provisions so that we might appreciate the totality of God's blessings that include our past, the present, and His promises for the future. In Hebrew, the word for gratitude is *hakarat hatov*, which literally means "recognizing the good." Thankfulness begins with awareness — awareness of what we have, of what God has done for us, and of what He continues to do for us each and every day. We can have all of the "good" in the world, but if we are not aware of it, if we do not recognize it, we cannot appreciate it.

Shavuot comes just once a year, but its message resonates all year no matter what season of life we might be in. It begins by recognizing the blessings in our life just as the ancient Israelites took notice of the first of their fruit beginning to blossom. It continues with expressing gratitude to God just as the Israelites did when they presented their fruit in the Temple. It concludes with truly enjoying everything that we have been given just as the firstfruits ceremony concluded with singing, feasting, and festivities. As the apostle Paul taught in the Christian Bible, "*give thanks in all circumstances; for this is God's will for you in Christ Jesus*" (1 Thessalonians 5:18).

———

Of all the Jewish practices that we can no longer observe because the Temple no longer exists, I believe the absence of the *bikurim* ceremony is one of the greatest losses. For thousands of years, as the Jews were banished from Jerusalem and the Temple remained demolished, the service was impossible. However, now that God has returned the Jews to Israel, the absence of the *bikurim* service is even more glaring. Once again, the Jewish people are building houses and growing the seven species of the land, just as the Bible prophesied. I can literally see the routes where the Israelites must have walked on their way to the Temple in Jerusalem as commanded in the Bible, and I can picture the beautiful procession of bringing the firstfruits. I can see it so clearly, and I have great faith that it will happen again soon.

... I recognize that the best way to teach my children to be grateful people in a world of entitlement is to model a grateful attitude myself.

However, during the two millennia when Jews lived exclusively in the Diaspora, the firstfruits ceremony was almost forgotten. Ultimately, Jewish children kept the ritual alive, as it became a tradition in many Jewish communities for them to reenact the joyful ceremony on *Shavuot*. Around the holiday, young children would come home from school with craft projects of beautiful baskets filled with fruit. They learned popular Hebrew children's songs about going to Jerusalem with firstfruits on their shoulders. Today, many children in Israel and around the world continue to reenact the long-forgotten ceremony. Our children dress in white, wear paper crowns adorned with flowers, and participate in a *bikurim* parade with their artfully made fruit baskets and festive music. It is a taste of what once was and what will be again. Most importantly, the children become familiar with the concept of celebrating and acknowledging God's blessings.

Fortunately, Judaism is replete with many traditions that help our children learn to be grateful throughout the year. Most prominently, the saying of blessings plays the biggest role in Judaism for training a grateful heart. In fact, the Jewish tradition is to recite no less than one hundred blessings a day! There are blessings for when we wake up, thanking God for another day. There is a blessing for going to the bathroom that thanks God for a functioning body. There are different blessings for different kinds of food that thank God for "the fruit of the tree," "the fruit of the ground," or "for bringing forth bread from the earth." Morning prayers include gratitude for the ability to see, the ability to walk, and the clothing we wear.

Many blessings are built into every day. When my children were small, my husband and I would recite every blessing aloud with our children. Since they learned to say them on their own, today they proudly recite them aloud, and we respond with an enthusiastic "Amen." My husband and I also make it a practice to thank each other aloud and often so that we create a "culture of gratitude" inside of our home. But of all the blessings and prayers we recite daily, the one that most closely resembles the message of the *bikurim* ceremony is the "Grace After Meals." Based on the biblical directive to praise God *"when you have eaten and are satisfied"* (Deuteronomy 8:10), Jews recite a prayer of thanksgiving *after* every meal. Many faith communities have the practice of reciting a grace before meals; however, Judaism is unique in the tradition of reciting grace *after* eating as well. This practice, like the bringing of the firstfruits, reminds us to bless God when we are satisfied and no longer hungry. At home and at school, my children recite the "Grace After Meals" following every meal.

Whether we have a little or a lot, where we put our focus makes the difference between feeling like we have less or feeling like we are abundantly blessed.

Ultimately, I recognize that the best way to teach my children to be grateful people in a world of entitlement is to model a grateful attitude myself. I make it a daily habit to practice *hakarat hatov*, to recognize the good in my life and to express genuine gratitude for all my many blessings. As a family, we take time to enjoy life and acknowledge our gifts. In this way a family excursion to the beach, a home-cooked meal shared together on *Shabbat*, or a trip to the mall for new shoes all become experiences of thankfulness.

Whether we have a little or a lot, where we put our focus makes the difference between feeling like we have less or feeling like we are abundantly blessed. It is my prayer that my children will be so filled with feelings of gratitude that they will be like a cup that runs over; they will simply have no room for negativity or entitlement while their grateful spirits spill onto everyone and everything that they encounter.

SHAVUOT IN THE NEW TESTAMENT

Christians encounter *Shavuot* in the New Testament, but with the name that is more familiar to them, Pentecost. Pentecost is the Greek word meaning "fifty," reflecting the seven weeks between Passover and the "Feast of the Weeks." Following his death and resurrection, Jesus' followers had gathered in Jerusalem in observance of this pilgrimage festival. Jesus had instructed them to wait there for the Father's gift of the Holy Spirit, which occurred on the very day of Pentecost, *Shavuot* (Acts 2). Christians in many churches today celebrate Pentecost as the birth of the church. Later in Acts 20:16, we read about Paul hurrying back to Jerusalem in order to be there for Pentecost. The concept of the firstfruits is also mentioned in the New Testament when Jesus himself is called the "firstfruit" in 1 Corinthians 15:20–23 and 2 Thessalonians 2:13.

Family Time — Teaching Our Children Gratitude

1. Discuss with your family what it means to bring God our "first-fruits" — our very best — in whatever we're doing. What does that look like at home? At work? At school? In the neighborhood?

2. Read the story of the widow's offering in Mark 12:41–44. What do the widow's actions reflect about her gratitude to God? How do they reflect giving her "firstfruits" to God?

3. Christian theologian Dietrich Bonhoeffer wrote, "It is only with gratitude that life becomes rich!" As a family, discuss what that means, and how you can put that into practice on a daily basis.

For Parents

Yael wrote, "Ultimately, I recognize that the best way to teach my children to be grateful people in a world of entitlement is to model a grateful attitude myself. I make it a daily habit to practice *hakarat hatov*, to recognize the good in my life and to express genuine gratitude for all my many blessings." What can you do to create a culture of gratitude in your family?

Memory Verses

Select one of the verses below on being grateful for you and your family to memorize.

Give thanks to the Lord, for he is good;
   his love endures forever. — 1 CHRONICLES 16:34

I will give thanks to you, Lord, with all my heart;
   I will tell of all your wonderful deeds. — PSALM 9:1

Let them give thanks to the Lord for his unfailing love
   and his wonderful deeds for mankind,
for he satisfies the thirsty
   and fills the hungry with good things. — PSALM 107:8-9

And whatever you do, whether in word or deed, do it all
   in the name of the Lord Jesus, giving thanks to God
   the Father through him. — COLOSSIANS 3:17

Rejoice always, pray continually, give thanks in all
   circumstances; for this is God's will for you in
   Christ Jesus. — 1 THESSALONIANS 5:16-18

TISHA B'AV

TEACHING OUR CHILDREN HOPE

Yet this I call to mind
and therefore I have hope:
Because of the LORD's great love we are not consumed,
for his compassions never fail.
They are new every morning;
great is your faithfulness. — LAMENTATIONS 3:21-23

"To be a Jew is to be an agent of
hope in a world serially threatened
by despair. Judaism is a sustained
struggle against the world that
is, in the name of the world that
could be, should be, but is not yet."

— *Rabbi Lord Jonathan Sacks, former Chief Rabbi of Great Britain*

ONE OF THE MOST REMARKABLE VIDEOS THAT WE HAVE OF
European Jews in the early 1930s is a group of children sing-
ing *Hatikvah*, written in the late 1800s by Naphtali Herz Imber, a
Jewish poet from Poland.

The children in the video had no idea that less than a decade
later most of them, along with their families, would be murdered by
the Nazis. They also had no clue that the very song they sang would
become the national anthem of a Jewish state that did not yet exist.
For the Jewish people, *Hatikvah* captures 2,000 years of exile and
our hope for the future. Its words:

As long as deep within the heart
A Jewish soul stirs,
And forward, to the ends of the East
An eye looks out, towards Zion.

Our hope is not yet lost,
The hope of two thousand years,
To be a free people in our land
The land of Zion and Jerusalem.

Two millennia of persecution could not break the Jewish spirit because of one powerful word: *Hatikvah*, "The Hope."

Holocaust survivor Elie Wiesel said, "Just as a man cannot live without dreams, he cannot live without hope." Hope is what has sustained the Jewish people through their long and bitter exile. Hope leaves room for God and His providence. Hope lets us believe that no matter how dark the world seems today, there can be a better tomorrow.

The prophet Jeremiah foresaw the difficult exile and described both the bitterness and the centrality of hope: "*I remember my affliction and my wandering, the bitterness and the gall ... Yet this I call to mind and therefore I have hope: Because of the LORD's great love we are not consumed, for his compassions never fail*" (Lamentations 3:19–22).

If we want our children to never give up and never give in when it comes to their values and beliefs, we must teach them hope. Hope is what led the bruised and battered nation of Israel back to our homeland, and it is hope that will lead our world to the Messianic Era.

I imagine that hope did not always come easily to the Jewish people. I grew up with a grandfather who survived the Holocaust that wiped out most of our family and one-third of the world's Jewish population. I cannot fathom how it was possible for any Jews to have hope for a future while thousands were gassed and cremated daily. It was the darkest chapter in Jewish history, and it is incomprehensible that anyone could see the light.

My grandfather told me countless stories about what happened to him and his family during the Holocaust. He grew up in Germany, and when it became apparent that the Nazis intended to exterminate the Jews, his family left all they had and fled. The family was fortunate enough to have a car, which they used to drive as far as they could to cross the border. At some point along the way, the car ran out of gas and they were stranded.

My great-grandmother stayed with my grandfather and his brother while their father went to look for gas. While he was gone, my great-grandmother and the boys heard the Nazis approaching.

They waited as long as they could for my great-grandfather to return, but when the bullets got too close, they ran. They left their car, the little belongings that they had, and their father and husband behind. It was terrifying.

When things eventually quieted down, they were grateful to be alive and certain that my great-grandfather had been killed in the incident. Meanwhile, my great-grandfather had been on his way to get gas for the car when he was told that the Nazis were headed in the direction of his family. He abandoned the quest for fuel and ran to find his family and bring them to a safe place. By the time he got to the car, all he saw were shards of glass, bullets, and no sign of his family. He was certain that his family had been murdered.

Against the dark backdrop of the Holocaust, I learned to see the glimmer of light, no matter how faint, in every situation.

Still, he did not give up hope that perhaps they had survived, and while my great-grandmother tried to move on without her husband, a part of her refused to give up hope that just maybe he was alive. Each one held out the tiniest bit of hope that the other had survived, and eventually they found one another.

These were my bedtime stories growing up. Seared into my soul is the notion that no matter how hopeless a situation looks, there is *always* room for hope. Against the dark backdrop of the Holocaust, I learned to see the glimmer of light, no matter how faint, in every situation.

Years later, I would hear my father compare the aftermath of the Holocaust to Ezekiel's vision of the dry bones. After the *Shoah*, the Jewish people were decimated. Whole communities were utterly wiped out, and along with them, hundreds of learning institutions, millions of Jewish scholars, countless cultural centers, and the security that Jews once enjoyed living in this world. How could such a decimated people go on and live again?

And yet, from the ashes of the Holocaust, Israel rose to life.

Just three years after World War II ended, the state of Israel was declared an independent nation. The Jewish people returned to their ancient homeland, and immediately set to work to drain the swamps, make the deserts bloom, and bring life back to the Holy Land. The following decades saw a resurgence of Jewish life in Israel, and around the world in countries like the United States and Canada that took in Holocaust survivors and gave them a second chance at life.

By the time I was born, the Jewish state, the Israeli army, and religious freedom for Jews in most parts of the world were all givens. I never knew a time without them. Nevertheless, I also never forgot the stories I heard firsthand from my grandfather about what had happened in the terrible years before. This has always been the Jewish way — to hope for the future while remembering our painful history.

Once a year, my family and I would join Jews around the world in our yearly mourning for the destruction of the Holy Temples and every tragedy the Jews have experienced ever since on *Tisha B'Av*. This day has been mourned for thousands of years — for centuries during which there seemed to be no end in sight to the long and painful suffering. However, from my perspective, although I fasted as the adults did (starting when I was 12, after my *bat mitzvah*) and felt the sad energy of the day, I could not help but also feel a sliver of joy. Yes, we have suffered; yes, we faced challenges; but oh, how far we had come and how brightly God's providence has been demonstrated to His children over and over again. That ray of light amidst the darkness formed my hope for the future and a vision of redemption.

It may sound strange at first, but it is on *Tisha B'Av*, the darkest day on the Jewish calendar, that we truly experience hope. Just as it takes the darkest skies to see the brightest stars, it is on this black day that we can experience the greatest light.

⌐━

Tisha B'Av, literally, the ninth of *Av*, is the saddest day of the Jewish year. Both the First and Second Temples were destroyed on *Tisha B'Av*. With the destruction of the Second Temple by the Romans in

70 CE, the Jews of Israel were dispersed to the *"four corners of the earth,"* setting in motion an exile whose ramifications are still felt today. But those are not the only tragedies to occur on this date.

On *Tisha B'Av* in 135 CE, the final Jewish rebellion against the Romans in the Holy Land was squelched and hundreds of Jews were brutally butchered. Exactly one year later, the Temple Mount was razed so that a pagan temple could be erected in its stead. In 1290 on *Tisha B'Av*, the Jews were expelled from England. In 1492 on *Tisha B'Av*, the Jews were kicked out of Spain. World War II and the Holocaust were the direct results of World War I, which — you guessed it — began on July 28, 1914, *Tisha B'Av*.

Through the darkness, there is a ray of light, a glimmer of hope, a glance into the future.

On this night, Jewish communities read the book of Lamentations, which begins *"Eicha ...,"* literally, "How can it be?" We lament the dramatic change that the Jewish people underwent when they were exiled from their land and the Temple was destroyed. Jerusalem, once the city of joy, had been transformed into a city in mourning. The Jewish people, once admired, esteemed, and a great spiritual people, were reduced to exiles, poor and helpless. Most tragic of all was the shattered relationship with the God of Israel — when once, the Jews enjoyed a unique and powerful connection to the Lord as His chosen people, His special treasure, the apple of His eye.

We cry out, "How can it be?" How can it be that the Jewish people went through the Holocaust, the single most devastating event in their long history of suffering? How can it be that after so many years, we still have not restored our relationship with God? How can it be that the world still has so much evil within it? As we read in Lamentations: *"This is why I weep and my eyes overflow with tears"* (1:16). On this one day each year, we acknowledge and cry for every calamity there has ever been.

Following the book of Lamentations, we recite elegies describing the many tragedies that have befallen the Jewish people throughout the centuries. On *Tisha B'Av*, we observe the laws of mourning, including sitting on low chairs, not greeting one another, and not wearing any freshly laundered clothing. In addition, Jewish adults do not eat or drink, engage in marital relations, wear leather shoes, shower, or apply soothing oils. The general atmosphere is somber, and we refrain from any physical activities that give us pleasure.

However, *Tisha B'Av* is not all about tragedy and mourning. Through the darkness, there is a ray of light, a glimmer of hope, a glance into the future. As we mourn what we lost in the past, we look toward what God has in store for us in the future.

A story is recorded in the *Talmud* (Judaism's Oral Tradition) that took place after the destruction of the Second Temple on the ninth of Av, 70 CE. Rabbi Akiva and his colleagues traveled to

Mount Scopus and witnessed the Temple's destruction. They were so distraught that they tore their clothing in mourning. When they got to the Temple Mount itself and saw foxes running around where the Holy of Holies once stood, they cried. However, Akiva laughed.

"Why are you laughing?" the rabbis asked. "Why are you crying?" Akiva replied. Incredulously, the rabbis explained that they were looking at the holiest place in the world and, now foxes run through it! "How could we not cry!" they exclaimed. "That is why I am laughing," Akiva answered. He continued, "One prophet said, '*because of you, Zion will be plowed like a field*' [Micah 3:12]. Another prophet said, '*once again men of women of ripe old age will sit in the streets of Jerusalem, each of them with cane in hand because of their age. The city streets will be filled with boys and girls playing there.*' [Zechariah 8:4–5]. Since the words of one prophet have been fulfilled, I now know that the words of the other prophet will also be fulfilled."

To this the rabbis exclaimed, "You have comforted us, Akiva, you have comforted us."

In the book of Lamentations, recited on *Tisha B'Av*, we further read: "*Let him bury his face in the dust — there may yet be hope*" (Lamentations 3:29). While we mourn on this day, it is also a day of hope. The tears that we shed on this day water the seeds of redemption; we pray, "*Those who sow with tears will reap with songs of joy*" (Psalm 126:5).

This is why, for all of the mournful elements of the day, *Tisha B'Av* is officially recognized as a holiday. Lamentations 1:15 reads, *"The LORD has rejected all my strong men in my midst; he has called an appointed time against me to crush my young men"* (NASB). The Hebrew term for "appointed time" is *moed*, which is reserved exclusively for describing holidays.

What is there to possibly celebrate on this day? The answer is hope.

According to Jewish tradition, the cherubs on the Holy Ark in the Temple represented God and Israel. When the relationship between God and Israel was strong, they faced each other; however when it was not, they faced away from each other. On the day that the Temple was destroyed, surprisingly, the cherubs were found in a loving embrace. This signified that although God destroyed the Temple, He would always love Israel, feel their pain, and carry them through difficult times. He would neither destroy His people nor desert them, and would accompany them into exile. Ultimately, God would return His nation to Israel and rebuild the Temple, as He had promised.

In Zechariah 8:19 we read: *"The fasts of the fourth, fifth, seventh and tenth months will become joyful and glad occasions and happy festivals for Judah."* The fast days mentioned in the verse are all connected to events that led up to the destruction of the Temple on the ninth of *Av*. God promised that these days are destined to be transformed into holidays. In fact, Jewish tradition teaches that *Tisha B'Av* is also the birthday of the messiah.

The holiday quality of *Tisha B'Av* reminds us that, ultimately, God will restore what we have lost. In other words, there is hope for the future. Mourning for the first two Temples creates a yearning for the Third Temple and gives us hope that one day there will be a world where evil does not exist.

Every year, before the sun sets on the 8th of *Av*, our family sits down to a meal. Unlike other holiday meals, instead of dessert, we end with traditional mourning food — a piece of bread with an egg dipped in ashes. The ashes symbolize the tragedies that we are about to mourn; however, the egg, with its circular shape, also reminds us that nothing — even the worst of times — lasts forever.

Once the sun sets, *Tisha B'Av* begins. My husband and I bring our children to the synagogue where we mourn as a community. We leave our jewelry and leather shoes behind and wear simple clothing and shoes. At the synagogue, we enter quietly and refrain from greeting friends. We sit on the floor in darkness, and with a flashlight in hand, we follow along as the book of Lamentations is recited aloud to the traditional melancholy tune.

Naturally, when my children were old enough to understand, they asked us why we do all of these strange things. This provides the opportunity to teach them about hope. We teach our children that while our focus is on gratitude, contentment, and joyfulness the rest of the year, we take one day to think about and express our emotions about all the things that make us sad. We are allowed to be angry with God. We are permitted — even encouraged — to question His ways. We are allowed to be sad about the tragedies that are part of life. There is only one emotion that we cannot feel — despair.

When we teach our children that this isn't the way the world is supposed to be, we teach them that, indeed, there is always hope; this world will not always be broken.

Children know that we do not live in a perfect world. They see the brokenness all around them. People get sick. Unexpected disasters such as floods and fires and earthquakes occur all too frequently. There are kids that go hungry, families that are falling apart, children in Israel who must run to bomb shelters, terror attacks, hate crimes, mass shootings … the list goes on and on. But as people of faith, we believe that this is not how the world is supposed to be. We believe that we are on a journey toward a perfect world.

All year round, I give my children the tools that they need in order to deal with the difficulties and challenges they face in life. I teach them resilience, how to find the positive aspects, and to have faith in God and His plans. I teach them to pray to our almighty God and to consider how we might help make the world a better place. On *Tisha B'Av*, I teach my children an entirely different lesson. I tell them that our broken world is unacceptable. It is not the way God intended our world to be, and it is not the way that things will always be. We can never get used to the way things are or settle for a less-than-perfect world.

By engaging in these yearly customs of mourning, our children — no matter what age — can grasp the sense that something is not right. They can tell that people are sad — unusually sad. It's not rare that adults cry during the *Tisha B'Av* service. I still remember in my childhood hearing the sobbing of Holocaust survivors in the synagogue.

> Hope is a foundational idea in both the Jewish and Christian faiths. In fact, it has been argued that Judaism brought the concept of hope to the world in the first place.

As children get older and begin to understand the sadness that is related to the loss of the Temple, they also begin to embrace the possibility of a Third Temple and a better world. If not for *Tisha B'Av*, it is highly unlikely that we would remember that there was a

Temple and that there will be a Temple rebuilt again in Jerusalem, and the significance of God's Holy Temple in our midst.

When we teach our children that this isn't the way the world is supposed to be, we teach them that, indeed, there is always hope; this world will not always be broken. The Temple will be rebuilt, the messiah will come, and our souls will be complete. In the Scriptures we read, "*Return to your fortress, you prisoners of hope; even now I announce that I will restore twice as much to you*" (Zechariah 9:12). We are prisoners of hope, captive to our faith, confined by our trust in God. What a beautiful word picture to instill in our children!

Hope is a foundational idea in both the Jewish and Christian faiths. In fact, it has been argued that Judaism brought the concept of hope to the world in the first place. When the biblical Abraham lived, the prevailing belief was that the "gods" determined man's fate. People had no control in changing their destiny. Their fate was left in the hands of the capricious gods. Abraham, however, taught of a loving God with whom anything is possible. Abraham and Sarah, who had their son Isaac at ages 90 and 100 respectively, proved that point. No matter how terrible or impossible a situation may seem, there is always room for hope.

In the book of Exodus, the very foundation of the Exodus story is that the Israelites cried out to God because of their suffering. God heard and intervened. Their situation seemed hopeless, but the Israelites demonstrated that the God of Israel is a God of hope. There is no room in faith for despair.

Rabbi Jonathan Sacks wrote, "Despair is not a Jewish emotion. *Od lo avda tikvatenu* (the Hebrew words from *Hatikvah*): our hope has never been destroyed. For there is a Jewish way of telling the story of our situation ... What happens is not chance but a chapter in the complex script of the covenant which leads, mysteriously but assuredly, to our redemption."

TISHA B'AV IN THE NEW TESTAMENT

As *Tisha B'Av* was added as a *moed*, "appointed time," only after the destruction of the Second Temple in 70 CE, Jesus clearly would not have observed this holiday. Yet, we do know that Jesus mourned for the city of Jerusalem. In Matthew 23:37, we read his lament: "*Jerusalem, Jerusalem, you who kill the prophets and stone those sent to you, how often I have longed to gather your children together, as a hen gathers her chicks under her wings, and you were not willing.*" Luke recorded that as Jesus and his disciples approached Jerusalem in the final week before Jesus' arrest and crucifixion, Jesus saw the city ahead of him and began to cry because he foresaw the destruction that was to come. (See Luke 19:41–44).

FAMILY TALK — TEACHING OUR CHILDREN HOPE

1. Ask your family what makes the hope described in the Bible different from other types of hope, such as "I hope we can go to the beach this weekend" or "I hope that I will get that special present I want for my birthday"?

2. Read the story of Abraham and God's promise to him in Genesis 12:1–3, and then Genesis 15:1–6. What did God promise Abraham? Why was Abraham so concerned in Genesis 15? What happened after God reaffirmed His promise to Abraham?

3. Christian theologian and author John Piper described biblical hope as "a confident expectation and desire for something good in the future." As a family, discuss what it means to have "a confident expectation." How did Abraham show "confident expectation"?

For Parents

Yael wrote, "We teach our children that while our focus is on gratitude, contentment, and joyfulness the rest of the year, we take one day to think about and express our emotions about all the things that make us sad." How can you help your children express their emotions about living in a broken world?

MEMORY VERSE

Select one of the verses below for you and your family to memorize
on the value of hope.

"For I know the plans I have for you," declares the LORD,
"plans to prosper you and not to harm you, plans to
give you hope and a future." — JEREMIAH 29:11

Yet this I call to mind
and therefore I have hope:
Because of the LORD's great love we are not consumed,
for his compassions never fail.
They are new every morning;
great is your faithfulness. — LAMENTATIONS 3:21-23

"With man this is impossible, but with God all
things are possible." — MATTHEW 19:26

And hope does not put us to shame, because God's love
has been poured out into our hearts through the Holy
Spirit, who has been given to us. — ROMANS 5:5

L'DOR V'DOR

HIGH HOLY DAYS

TEACHING OUR CHILDREN FORGIVENESS

"You shall not hate your brother in your heart, but you shall reason frankly with your neighbor, lest you incur sin because of him." — LEVITICUS 19:17 (ESV)

Who is a God like you,
  who pardons sin and forgives the transgression
  of the remnant of his inheritance?
You do not stay angry forever
  but delight to show mercy. — MICAH 7:18

I hereby forgive all who have transgressed against me, whether on purpose or by accident, whether in this lifetime or on any other plane ... . Let no one be punished on my account.

— *Hareni Mochel prayer before the evening Shema*

MANY OF US BEAR EMOTIONAL BAGGAGE THAT WE CARRY throughout our lives. It's the type of baggage that can slow us down, throw us off balance, and even threaten our mental well-being, just as carrying too much physical weight can. Yet, the truth is that many of the burdens we bear are burdens we could put down if we wanted to, instead of endlessly suffering from them on a daily basis.

Specifically, most of us carry two types of baggage. One is the need for forgiveness. This baggage contains guilt, shame, hopelessness, and sadness. The other is the need to forgive. This baggage is filled with anger, resentment, regret, and turmoil. Both have the power to prevent us from true personal and spiritual growth. Ridding ourselves of these burdens is freeing, and ultimately, life changing, yet neither is easy to put down.

In order to obtain forgiveness, we must be willing to humble ourselves and have the courage to admit wrongdoing. In order to forgive a person who has hurt us, we have to be willing to let go of the past and overlook another person's wrongdoings. Moreover, the need to forgive and to be forgiven are not only issues with other people. They are also deep needs relating to both God and ourselves. There is not a person on earth who does not need God's forgiveness. The Bible tells us that, *"Indeed, there is no one on earth who is righteous, no one who does what is right and never sins"* (Ecclesiastes 7:20). As the apostle Paul wrote in the Christian Bible, *"for all have sinned and fall short of the glory of God"* (Romans 3:23). In addition, often the person we most need to forgive is ourselves.

Forgiveness is difficult, but its rewards are invaluable. We find forgiveness at the heart of some of the most pivotal events of Israel's history in the Bible. One of the most impactful and emotional stories in the Bible is when Joseph forgave his brothers for what they had done to him. In Genesis 50:15, after their father Jacob had died, the brothers were terrified that without their father's protection, Joseph would take revenge upon them. Yet, Joseph had forgiven his brothers long ago, and in some of the most powerful words of forgiveness ever uttered, he reassured them, *"Don't be afraid. Am I in the place of God? You intended to harm me, but God intended it for* *good to accomplish what is now being done, the saving of many lives.* *So then, don't be afraid. I will provide for you and your children"* (Genesis 50:19–21). Imagine what the fate of the nation of Israel would be if Joseph had not forgiven his brothers?

> Even though it has been scientifically proven that seeking forgiveness is immensely beneficial, two of the hardest words for many people to say are, "I'm sorry."

Fast-forward to another critical moment in the history of Israel, when Moses pleaded with God to forgive the children of Israel for building and bowing down before a golden calf while he was on Mount Sinai receiving God's law: *"Turn from your fierce* *anger; relent and do not bring disaster on your people"* (Exodus 32:12). Then once again, Moses pleaded for forgiveness on behalf of the people as they stood on the threshold of the Promised Land and refused to enter because they were afraid. Moses said, *"In accor-* *dance with your great love, forgive the sin of these people, just as* *you have pardoned them from the time they left Egypt until now"* (Numbers 14:19). And God replied, *"I have forgiven them, as you* *asked"* (Numbers 14:20). If not for God's grace, the nation of Israel would not have received the Ten Commandments, become God's chosen nation, or inherited the Holy Land.

Asking forgiveness, giving forgiveness, and attaining forgiveness are critical to living a healthy and happy life. As Jesus taught his disciples in the Christian Bible, "*For if you forgive other people when they sin against you, your heavenly Father will also forgive you. But if you do not forgive others their sins, your Father will not forgive your sins*" (Matthew 6:14–15). Forgiveness is not only good for the souls of others; it is good for our soul as well.

—

Even though it has been scientifically proven that seeking forgiveness is immensely beneficial, two of the hardest words for many people to say are, "I'm sorry." Those two words have tremendous power to heal relationships, repair damages, and change the future for the better. Yet so many people would rather live with the pain of brokenness then say those words aloud. People often mistake the act of apology as a sign of weakness or as an act of submission to another person. However, nothing could be further from the truth.

It takes a strong person to ask for forgiveness. It requires courage and inner strength to put one's self into such a vulnerable position. It requires humility to admit doing wrong, and paradoxically, a good sense of self-worth in order to know that such an admission does not diminish one's value. Apologies are not for the weak.

Sincere apologies take a person who is strong enough to lower his or her self in front of another person, to feel remorse, to express regret, and to accept responsibility for his or her actions. No one taught me this lesson better than my father did.

I remember a time when I was a child, and I was not behaving well. I was acting out and speaking inappropriately to my parents as children often do. My father told me to stop misbehaving once, twice, a third time. Nevertheless, I kept on what I was doing, caught up in my own world, and barely paying attention to my father's gentle reprimand. My father sensed that I was completely ignoring him, and consequently was upset and yelled at me. This was something that I was not used to, and it scared me. My father didn't get angry with me very often and rarely expressed it the way that he did on that day. I ran to my room in tears.

… in addition to accepting God as our King and Judge, on this holiday we also relate to God as our loving Father and recall His great mercy.

A few moments later, I heard my father's footsteps coming up the stairs. He came into my room and sat on my bed where I had buried my face in my pillow. I realized that I had been misbehaving and thought that maybe my father had come to punish me. But that's not what happened.

Instead, my father stroked my back until I stopped sobbing and looked up at him. With tears in his eyes he said, "I'm sorry, Yael. I should not have reacted so harshly. Yes, you were misbehaving, but you are the child and I am the parent. I should not have lost my cool and yelled at you. There are other ways that I could have dealt with it, and in the future, I am going to be more patient and talk things out with you."

I could hardly believe it. My towering, big, strong, father, who was larger than life, had come to apologize to me! In my eyes, my father was always right and never made mistakes. It was incredibly powerful when he admitted to me that he had been wrong and apologized for the way that he reacted (even though I definitely deserved it!). I remember thinking that everyone makes mistakes, even my father, and that everyone can, and should, apologize when they do. That day I learned that the sign of a truly strong and mature adult is the ability to ask forgiveness from anyone, even a small child. I learned that it was not just the "right" thing to do, but it also was the hallmark of a great person.

In life, we all make mistakes, but a righteous person corrects them. In Judaism, the highest form of repentance is when a person is in the exact same situation as when they first sinned and they choose a different course of action. After my father apologized for losing his temper with me, he found himself in the same position many, many times throughout my childhood. However, every time I pushed him to the limit, he would say to me, "Remember that promise that I made to you, Yael, to not lose my cool and yell at you? Let's sit down and talk about this."

Every time that my father reminded me of his promise, he also taught me the value of a true, sincere apology. Such an apology can change our destiny and transform us into the best versions of ourselves.

———

The most sacred time on the Jewish calendar is known as the High Holidays, or the High Holy Days, which begin with *Rosh Hashanah*, literally the "Head of the Year" and commonly referred to as the Jewish New Year, and culminate on *Yom Kippur*, the Day of Atonement. The two holidays are connected by the days between them, known as the Ten Days of Repentance. This is a time of intense introspection, self-reflection, and repentance that leads to *asking* forgiveness from God and also *seeking* forgiveness from those whom we have hurt or offended — whether intentionally or unintentionally — throughout the year. It is a time we can chart a new course and begin the year with a clean slate.

These holy days are a delicate balance between feasting and fasting, repenting and rejoicing. According to Jewish tradition, *Rosh Hashanah* is a day of judgment when God takes a close look at every person — his or her deeds, misdeeds, their heart, and their truest intentions — and makes an assessment. It's our yearly spiritual checkup. The Bible refers to *Rosh Hashanah* as "The Festival of Trumpets," a reference to the ritual ram's horn known as the *shofar* that we sound throughout the two-day holiday (Leviticus 23:23–25). The *shofar* serves as an alarm clock that reminds us to wake up from our spiritual slumber, evaluate ourselves, repent where necessary, and return to God. The trumpet blasts are also a reference to royalty and symbolize our yearly re-coronation of God as our King and our rededication to Him as His subjects. However, in addition to accepting God as our King and Judge, on this holiday we also relate to God as our loving Father and recall His great mercy. *Rosh Hashanah* is both a solemn day and a day of celebration because God is merciful and forgives our sins. According to Jewish tradition, when we appear for Divine judgment, the angels say, "Don't be afraid, the Judge is your Father."

The High Holy Days are our opportunity to wipe the slate clean, and begin the year anew — with new dreams, possibilities, intentions, and commitments.

The themes of introspection, repentance, and forgiveness continue through the days between *Rosh Hashanah* and *Yom Kippur*. These days are considered an ideal time for sincere repentance, as Jews believe that God is especially close and attentive to our prayers. The Ten Days of Repentance lead up to the culmination of the High Holy Day season on *Yom Kippur*, the Day of Atonement.

Historically, *Yom Kippur* was the day that Moses attained forgiveness on behalf of the Israelites for the sin of the golden calf. It is considered an auspicious day for forgiveness for all time. In Temple times, *Yom Kippur* centered around a service laid out in detail in Leviticus 16, and was the only day of the year that the High Priest entered the Holy of Holies and made atonement for the sins of the nation. As God commanded, *"on this day atonement will be made for you, to cleanse you. Then, before the* LORD, *you will be clean from all your sins"* (Leviticus 16:30).

Divine forgiveness is a gift from God that must be valued and appreciated.

Today, the Day of Atonement is marked primarily by fasting, praying, and asking for God's forgiveness. In spite of the very somber aspects of the day, some have also called it one of the happiest days on the Jewish calendar. Moses Ibn Ezra, an 11th-century Jewish scholar, explained, "No sin is so light that it may be overlooked. No sin is so heavy that it may not be repented of." On *Yom Kippur*, we are serious about confronting our shortcomings and joyful that our God is a merciful God, a God who forgives and can completely erase our sins as though they never happened.

The High Holy Days are our opportunity to wipe the slate clean, and begin the year anew — with new dreams, possibilities, intentions, and commitments. We enter the New Year with greater wisdom, higher aspirations, and a renewed relationship with God. As Christian theologian Billy Graham once said, "Every year during their High Holy Days, the Jewish community reminds us all of our need for repentance and forgiveness."

According to the Jewish Oral Tradition, God created the possibility of repentance before He even created the world. This is because repentance goes against the rules of nature. The laws of nature dictate that once something is broken, it cannot be put back together. Once glass is shattered, even the most talented artisan cannot mend it. Moreover, we cannot travel back in time to prevent the glass from being shattered in the first place. However, through repentance, God created a way for us to do both — to fix what has been broken and to change the past, so to speak, making it as if the breaking never happened in the first place. God's forgiveness is nothing less than a miracle — it goes against the laws of nature so that we can be redeemed.

Divine forgiveness is a gift from God that must be valued and appreciated. "The single most important lesson of *Yom Kippur*," writes Rabbi Jonathan Sacks, "is that it's never too late to change, start again, and live differently from the way we've done in the past. God forgives every mistake we've made so long as we are honest in regretting it and doing our best to put it right."

As the *Yom Kippur* liturgy asserts, there is no such thing as a person who does not sin. However, sin can only hold us back if we let it. God has given us the power to release ourselves from the tentacles of sin by asking forgiveness and resolving to behave differently in the future. God promises, *"If my people who are called by my name, will humble themselves and pray and seek my face and turn from their wicked ways, then I will hear from heaven, and I will forgive their sin and heal their land"* (2 Chronicles 7:14). The pathway back to God is always open.

Yet, Judaism maintains that there are sins which God cannot forgive — at least not without a critical step before we ask for His grace. When it comes to our relationship with God, He can forgive anything. But God does not forgive our wrongdoings to other human beings until we have asked for forgiveness from the person or people we have harmed. True repentance, when it comes to other people, requires a sincere apology and a significant attempt to set things right. For this reason, it has become customary for Jewish people to seek forgiveness from family, friends, and anyone they may have harmed, just before the High Holy Days. We apologize for our wrongdoings, big or small, and grant forgiveness to others before we seek forgiveness from God.

The High Holy Days are not only about seeking forgiveness; they are also a time to let go of the past and forgive others. In the Jewish Oral Tradition, a story is told about a first-century rabbi who prayed for rain during a time of drought in the Holy Land, yet his prayers were not answered. However, when his student prayed for rain, it started to rain immediately. While the other sages present were trying to figure out why the student's prayer was answered and the great sage's prayer was not, a heavenly voice called out that it was not an issue of greatness; rather, the student was more open and forgiving, while the teacher was more exact and demanding. God responded to each of them according to his personality.

Rather than harbor a grudge and resentment, we must make every attempt to work things out with those we feel have hurt us.

While we are not permitted to forgive someone on behalf of another individual, nor are we required to forgive someone as they continue to harm us, we must be willing to forgive those who have hurt us when they sincerely apologize. Indeed, it has been said that holding on to resentment is like drinking poison and hoping the other person will die. Yet, aside from the freedom we receive from forgiving others, we also invoke God's forgiveness and mercy when we are merciful toward others. Furthermore, we are commanded,

"You shall not hate your brother in your heart" (Leviticus 19:17 ESV). Rather than harbor a grudge and resentment, we must make every attempt to work things out with those we feel have hurt us. Just as we must pursue forgiveness for ourselves, we must also seek to forgive others. As the apostle Paul taught in the Christian Bible, *"Bear with each other and forgive one another if any of you has a grievance against someone. Forgive as the Lord forgave you"* (Colossians 3:13)

When it comes to forgiving others, I can honestly say that my children have been my teachers at least as much as I have been theirs. By nature, our children can more easily let go of anger and move on quickly after someone else has hurt them. When we are young, we do not have the mental faculties to ruminate over an unpleasant interaction or the memory capacity to keep past incidents in the forefront of our minds for years to come. As we age and our minds mature, we gain the tools to analyze and remember our experiences, but if we are not careful, they can get in our way when it comes to forgiving and letting go of the past. Forgiving does not mean forgetting, but it does provide freedom.

There was one time in particular that my daughter taught me the power of letting go. She was three years old when she asked me for a candy that she saw on a shelf and I told her "no." Needless to say, she was not very happy about that answer. She threw a classic tantrum, crying and protesting the situation, which I am sure from her perspective was unfair and unkind. But then she did something interesting. Just a few moments later, she climbed into my lap and snuggled up against my chest.

When we can separate our circumstances from the persons or people who played a role in creating them, we can more easily forgive and move on.

My daughter's reaction taught me two things. First, that it is possible to separate a situation from a person. She was upset at her circumstances, but she dropped her anger at me. Part of faith means believing that our lives are exactly as they are meant to be no matter who or what contributed to them. When we can separate our circumstances from the person or people who played a role in creating them, we can more easily forgive and move on. The second concept that my daughter's actions illustrated was the power of moving on quickly and completely. Wallowing in her pity and anger would not have served her well. Focusing on our loving relationship allowed her to unburden herself from the pain of resentment and step into love. Of course, she did not do any of this consciously; it comes more naturally to a child. Yet, as adults, we have the opportunity to do the same intentionally.

A beautiful Jewish prayer included in the nighttime prayers we say just before going to sleep illustrates the power of forgiveness. The prayer is both a declaration that we forgive anyone that may have hurt us in any way and a request that we be forgiven, as well. It reads:

> Master of the Universe, I hereby forgive anyone who has angered or antagonized me or who sinned against me — whether against my body, my property, my honor, or against anything of mine; whether he did so accidentally, willfully, carelessly, or purposely; whether through speech, deed, thought, or notion; whether in this lifetime or another lifetime — I forgive everyone. May no man be punished because of me. May it be Your will LORD, my God and the God of my forefathers, that I may sin no more. Whatever sins that I have done before you, may You blot out in your abundant mercies, but not through suffering or bad illnesses. May the expressions of my mouth and the thoughts of my heart find favor before You, God, my Rock and Redeemer.

The intention of this prayer is that we never go to bed angry, not only for the sake of those who have hurt us, but also for ourselves. Every morning is a fresh start to a new day. Carrying over past hurt and resentment only holds us back from enjoying God's blessings. When I say this prayer with my children at night, my hope is that their natural tendency to forgive will accompany them throughout their lives, and that they will grow into forgiving and merciful adults who are kind to others and to themselves.

Asking for forgiveness, however, does not come as easily, and our children need to be taught how to incorporate this into their spiritual development. Nobody likes to admit being wrong. Yet, like most parents, my husband and I have insisted that our children apologize as sincerely as possible when they are wrong. Having 40 days out of every year when our entire faith community focuses on asking forgiveness from God and from others has helped immeasurably in guiding my children to be comfortable with apologizing. For the entire month before *Rosh Hashanah*, we observe the tradition to sound the ritual *shofar* every day in our home. The piercing sound and unusual-looking trumpet captured our children's attention from a very young age. As they grow older, they automatically associate the sound of the *shofar* with repentance and asking forgiveness.

As the New Year approaches, asking forgiveness becomes commonplace. It is common in Jewish schools that principals, teachers, and other authority figures in the lives of our children ask for forgiveness in case they inadvertently hurt a child's feelings. Imagine the impact that has upon a child — seeing the adults and authorities in their lives humbly asking for forgiveness — much like the impact my father had on me when I was a child. In addition, my children and their friends will exchange apologies in advance of the holidays. While the apologies may come more from a place of tradition instead of sincere regret, this practice trains our children to ask forgiveness and to forgive. It gives them the tools to become mature adults who are able to humble themselves when they are wrong and make amends, just as my father did.

HIGH HOLY DAYS IN THE NEW TESTAMENT

Neither *Rosh Hashanah* nor *Yom Kippur* are mentioned specifically in the New Testament; however, the underlying themes found in these observances are evident. For example, the call to repentance as symbolized by the sounding of the *shofar* on *Rosh Hashanah* is found repeatedly in New Testament scriptures. As Jesus began his ministry, John the Baptist prepared the way by announcing, *"Repent, for the kingdom of heaven has come near"* (Matthew 3:2). Certainly, repentance was a key message in Jesus' and his followers' teachings (Matthew 3:2; 4:17; Mark 6:12; Luke 5:32; Acts 2:38). Additionally, the New Testament makes many comparisons between the Day of Atonement and the sacrificial death of Jesus (Hebrews 9:6–28; 13:11–13).

FAMILY TIME — TEACHING OUR CHILDREN FORGIVENESS

1. As a family, write down (or share) something for which you need forgiveness. Then write down someone who you need to forgive. Which is the harder thing to do?

2. Read the following parable Jesus taught his disciples about forgiveness in Matthew 18:23–35. What does this teach about how God views forgiveness? How should we treat others who have wronged us?

3. Frederick Robertson, a 19th-century British Anglican clergyman, wrote, "We win by tenderness. We conquer by forgiveness." As a family, discuss what that means and what it teaches us about the need to forgive one another.

For Parents

In discussing the *Hareni Mochel*, the traditional prayer of forgiveness she and her children say each night, Yael wrote, "When I say this prayer with my children at night, my hope is that their natural tendency to forgive will accompany them throughout their lives, and that they will grow into forgiving and merciful adults who are kind to others and to themselves." How might you incorporate a prayer for forgiveness with your children on a regular basis?

MEMORY VERSES

Select one of the verses below for you and your family to memorize on forgiveness.

> *"I, even I, am he who blots out*
> > *your transgressions, for my own sake,*
> > *and remembers your sins no more."* —ISAIAH 43:25

> *Who is a God like you,*
> > *who pardons sin and forgives the transgression*
> > *of the remnant of his inheritance?*
> *You do not stay angry forever*
> > *but delight to show mercy.* —MICAH 7:18

> *"For if you forgive other people when they sin against*
> > *you, your heavenly Father will also forgive you. But*
> > *if you do not forgive others their sins, your Father*
> > *will not forgive your sins."* —MATTHEW 6:14-15

> *Bear with each other and forgive one another if any of*
> > *you has a grievance against someone. Forgive as*
> > *the Lord forgave you.* —COLOSSIANS 3:13

SUKKOT

Teaching Our Children Faith

Trust in the Lord with all your heart
  and lean not on your own understanding;
in all your ways submit to him,
  and he will make your paths straight. — PROVERBS 3:5-6

"But blessed is the one who trusts in the Lord,
  whose confidence is in him." — JEREMIAH 17:7

"Faith is not a series of theorems but a way of life."

— *Samuel Hugo Bergman, (1883–1975), 19th-century Israeli Philosopher*

FROM GOD'S COMMANDMENT TO ABRAHAM TO LEAVE HIS homeland for a land he did not know following a God that he could not see, to the nation of Israel standing on the shores of the Red Sea with the mighty Egyptian army at their heels, to the prophet Daniel facing certain death in the lion's den, the *Torah* is filled with stories and lessons about faith in God. In fact one of the greatest Jewish sages, the 18th-century Rabbi Elijah of Vilna, taught that the entire purpose of the Bible is, "*So that your trust may be in the LORD*" (Proverbs 22:19). Indeed, what is the purpose of any faith community if not to inspire faith in our heavenly Father?

However, upon closer examination, it is clear that there are different levels of faith. There is a foundational belief in God, including the conviction that He is all-knowing, all-powerful, and all-loving. In Jewish tradition, we affirm 13 principles of faith each day, such as our belief that God created the world and the belief that the messiah will come. Every day, we declare that we believe in God's existence and acknowledge His involvement in the world.

Yet, there is another type of faith, one which requires us to take what we believe in our head and unite it with our heart so that we live out our faith. This type of faith requires that we not only *believe* in God, but that we also *trust* God — day in and day out, moment to moment. The great 19th-century *Torah* scholar Rabbi Israel Salanter said, "The longest distance between two points is the distance between the head and the heart." These two levels of faith — between what we believe with our mind and know in our heart — are, indeed, often worlds apart. Bridging the two is part of our lifelong service to God. In the Christian Bible, the apostle Paul described it this way, "*For we live by faith, not by sight*" (2 Corinthians 5:7).

There is a wonderful story that illustrates this. Around the mid-1800s, a man known as the Great Blondin attempted to cross Niagara Falls on a tightrope. Five thousand people gathered to watch. In the middle of the walk, Blondin suddenly stopped, back-flipped into the air, landed on the rope, and then continued safely to the other side. Blondin would cross the Falls many more times — once blindfolded, once carrying a stove, once in chains, and once on a bicycle.

One time, however, he showed up with a wheelbarrow. Blondin turned to the crowd and shouted, "Who believes that I can cross pushing this wheelbarrow?" Every hand in the crowd went up.

Blondin pointed at one man. "Do you believe that I can do it?" he asked. "Yes, I believe you can," said the man. "Are you sure?" said Blondin. "Yes," said the man. "Absolutely certain?" "Yes, absolutely certain." "Thank you," said Blondin. "Then, sir, get into the wheelbarrow."

Anyone can have a belief, but how many of us are ready to stake our lives on what we believe? There will be times in our lives when our faith will be strong, but our fear will seem stronger. We will all have to decide if we are willing to step into the wheelbarrow and trust that God will deliver us safely across the wire.

In Judaism, there are two words that roughly express the idea of faith. One is *emunah*, the other is *bitachon*, and there is a profound difference between the two. *Emunah* is believing in God and that He runs the world. *Bitachon* is acting in accordance with that belief. For example, a butcher who believes that his earnings all come from God has *emunah*. However, if he panics when a competitor opens up shop, then he is lacking *bitachon*. *Bitachon* means knowing that only God determines how our lives will unfold and that everything that happens is for the best.

In Judaism, faith is really a verb; it is something we *do*, not something we *have*. It means living our lives in a way that is congruent with our belief in God and our trust in Him. Every year the Jewish people practice this faith-living on the holiday of *Sukkot*, the Feast of Tabernacles. For seven days, we leave the comfort of our homes and go live outside in a rickety hut called a *sukkah* as a reminder of God's provision and protection for us year-round. Just as God had protected the Israelites while they wandered the harsh desert following the Exodus, God provides and protects us while we live in vulnerable conditions.

> I learned that when things do not go according to plan, it does not mean that God is not in control or that He does not love me.

These days, there are many options when it comes to building a *sukkah*. There are pre-fab ones that are as easy to put together (and as fun) as LEGO® blocks and there are even "pop-up" versions. When I was growing up, our *sukkah* was made of wood, and I remember my sisters and I watching in awe as my father single-handedly constructed it.

This was no easy feat. First, my father would lug the wooden panels from our shed to our patio, along with the wooden beams that would hold the structure together. Then he would carefully line up the pieces according to the numbers he had assigned them the very first time he built our *sukkah*, so that everything was in place and ready to be assembled. The first two pieces were always the most difficult. My father would follow his plan carefully and join two boards in order to form a corner, which once bolted together, could stand on its own as long as there were no strong winds that day! My father worked as quickly as he could to stabilize the structure while my sisters and I were there to help by handing him the next screw or getting him a glass of water.

It was always a celebrated accomplishment when the *sukkah* was finally complete and stable enough to be decorated. We would sit with my father long after the sun had set and marvel at the structure that once again stood in our Chicago backyard. Over the following days, as is the custom, my sisters and I would hang decorations from the thatched roof and on the walls so that by the time the holiday began, we took great pride in our combined efforts to produce such a magnificent structure — a veritable palace in our young eyes.

One year, there was a powerful storm on the first night of *Sukkot*. We had finished our meal in the *sukkah* as the first drops of rain began to fall. Sleeping in the *sukkah* as we usually did was out of the question, and our family went to bed inside our "regular" home for the night. In the morning, we were distraught to see that our beloved *sukkah*, which we had worked so hard to build, had been blown down by the storm. Our decorations were ruined, and the *sukkah* was in pieces on the ground. My father sensed our sadness and said to us, "Girls, we will rebuild our *sukkah* and the rest of the holiday will be fine. But I want you to know that God just taught us a very important lesson about life. We can make plans and work hard, but in the end, only God decides what will happen. Even when we don't like how things turn out, we trust God that everything is for the best."

Looking back now, it's clear to me that God allowing our *sukkah* to fall was one of the best life lessons I ever received because it was on that day that I learned to truly trust God — to put my faith (*emunah*) into practice (*bitachon*). I learned that when things do not go according to plan, it does not mean that God is not in control or that He does not love me. I learned that I do not have to understand God's ways to know that He is always good. I learned the true meaning of the verse, "*For my thoughts are not your thoughts, neither are your ways my ways,' declares the* LORD" (Isaiah 55:8).

… God provided manna from the sky for them to eat, a traveling well of water for them to drink, and shelters to live in while they camped.

Every year after that when we built our *sukkah*, it was no more sturdy than the year it blew down, and many times the Chicago weather was just as bad or worse. Yet, it never blew down again. During those years, I learned that while God might have allowed our *sukkah* to fall apart once, He could also hold up the flimsy structure against all odds year after year. Even as our *sukkah* aged and the wood began to warp, it was not God's will for it to fall, and so it stood for decades.

———

The holiday of *Sukkot* is a celebration of *bitachon,* that very faith-living and trust in God. Also known as the Feast of Tabernacles or the Festival of Booths, the festival recalls the 40-year journey that the Israelites took across the desert after their Exodus from Egypt. During that time, God provided for His people in an environment where it is nearly impossible to survive. The Bible tells us that God provided a pillar of cloud during the day and a pillar of fire at night to guide His people (Exodus 13:21). In addition, God provided manna from the sky for them to eat, a traveling well of water for them to drink, and shelters to live in while they camped. On *Sukkot,* we remember all God's provisions for His children – as the psalmist reminds us, *"For in the day of trouble he will keep me safe in his dwelling; he will hide me in the shelter of his sacred tent and set me high upon a rock"* (Psalm 27:5).

In Leviticus 23:42–43, we are commanded to *"Live in temporary shelters for seven days: All native-born Israelites are to live in such shelters so your descendants will know that I had the Israelites live in temporary shelters when I brought them out of Egypt. I am the* LORD *your God."* On *Sukkot,* we live in a temporary hut, a *sukkah,* for an entire week to remember how God cared for and protected our ancestors in the desert during those 40 years. When God took the Israelites out of Egypt, He didn't just leave them to fend for themselves. He provided them with all their needs on a daily basis on their journey to the Promised Land. On *Sukkot*, we are reminded that God will also provide for us and that we can trust Him in all circumstances — be they times of deprivation and harshness, or of abundance and joy.

In truth, we always live by the grace of God. The difference is that all year long we create the illusion that we are in control of our destiny.

Sukkot is celebrated in the fall, just a few days after the High Holy Days of *Rosh Hashanah* and *Yom Kippur*. The Jewish custom is to begin building a *sukkah* immediately after *Yom Kippur* ends. The walls are usually constructed out of simple pieces of wood or from canvas, but the roof, called *schach*, must be created out of natural materials like bamboo or tree branches and must be sparse enough so that the stars can be seen from inside the structure. All year long, when we look up in our homes, we see the sturdy ceiling and roof as the source of our protection. But on *Sukkot*, within our *sukkah*, we look up and see the heavens, and know that our Savior and Protector is God.

During this holiday, we eat, sleep, and spend as much time as we can inside the holy *sukkah*. We try to make it resemble a home as much as possible, and we are encouraged to decorate it beautifully. Since *Sukkot* takes place during the harvest season — it originally marked the ingathering of the fall harvest as a thanksgiving festival — many people decorate the *sukkah* with hanging fruits (real or faux) of the seven species of the land of Israel, such as pomegranates, grapes, and figs.

Interestingly, although *Sukkot* is probably one of the lesser known of the Jewish holidays, it is described in the Bible as a holiday for all nations in the messianic era. The book of Zechariah tells us that *"the survivors from all the nations … will go up year after year to worship the King, the LORD Almighty, and to celebrate the Festival of Tabernacles"* (14:16). *Sukkot* has universal and eternal significance for people of all faith; as we read in the book of Zechariah in synagogue, *"The LORD will be king over the whole earth. On that day there will be one LORD, and his name the only name"* (14:9).

When we understand that *Sukkot* commemorates God's providence in the desert following the Exodus from Egypt (recalled on Passover, which occurs in the spring), an important question arises: Why isn't *Sukkot* celebrated in the springtime, the same season when its events originally took place?

According to Jewish tradition, *Sukkot* is celebrated in autumn so that we can experience God's providence while exposed to the elements, just as the ancient Israelites experienced His shelter and protection while exposed to the dangers of the desert. Autumn ushers in the time when most people move from outdoors to inside. The weather gets cooler, and in Israel, the rainy season begins.

There is no greater joy in life than having complete trust in God, knowing that everything was, is, and always will be exactly as it should be — divinely ordained, perfect, and for our very best.

However, instead of taking shelter inside our homes, under our sturdy roofs, it is precisely in this vulnerable environment that we move outside into our rickety, unstable *sukkah*. *Sukkot* tests our willingness to sacrifice our comfort and convenience for the sake of obedience and trust in God and His word.

The roof of a *sukkah* has to provide more shade than sun, but as mentioned previously, it must also be sparse enough to see the sky and let in rain. We want to be exposed. We want to have the experience of completely relying on God when we could perhaps more easily rely upon our manmade homes and ourselves. On *Sukkot*, we choose vulnerability. We relish the opportunity to live by the grace of God. And for this act of faith, the prophet Jeremiah declared, the Jewish people merited divine loving-kindness: "*I remember the devotion of your youth, you ... followed me through the wilderness, through a land not sown*" (2:2).

In truth, we always live by the grace of God. The difference is that all year long we create the illusion that we are in control of our destiny. We live in our big strong homes protected by locks and alarms. Many of us enjoy climate-controlled houses that provide us with comfort in the heat and the cold, and immunity from the weather. However, once we step into the *sukkah*, we realize that we are no longer in control. Our *sukkah* is intended to be a metaphor for life, reminding us that in spite of all the scientific and technological success that God has allowed us, we never have been — nor ever will be — in charge of our destiny. Only God holds the reins of the world — we live or die by His will alone.

In the Jewish Oral Tradition, the *sukkah* is referred to as a "shelter of faith." Houses rest upon strong physical foundations and rely upon human ability. A *sukkah,* in contrast, rests on faith alone and relies solely on God to protect the structure and the people within it. When we are in the *sukkah*, we are sitting in the "shadow of faith," and the walls of the structure are considered a divine embrace.

Sukkot is also known as the "time of our joy," based on the Bible verse that instructs us, "*Celebrate the Festival of Tabernacles ... Be joyful at your festival*" (Deuteronomy 16:13–14). There is no greater joy in life than having complete trust in God, knowing that everything was, is, and always will be exactly as it should be — divinely ordained, perfect, and for our very best.

Sukkot is definitely one of the most joyful weeks of the year for our family. The excitement begins the moment the sun sets on *Yom Kippur*. After breaking our fast at a family meal, we head into our yard and begin constructing our *sukkah*. The sound of nails being hammered into wood fills the neighborhood, mixed with the sound of children's laughter.

Once our *sukkah* is standing, our children begin to decorate it, just as my sisters and I used to do. They bring home school projects to hang on the walls of the *sukkah* and make paper chains out of colorful strips of paper to drape from the ceiling. As the holiday gets closer, the *schach* goes up, which in Israel is usually comprised of large palm fronds that are conveniently delivered to our home.

Once *Sukkot* begins, our family moves into the *sukkah*. There we eat, entertain family and friends, play music, sing, and enjoy each other's company. At night, we drag out mattresses and lay out sleeping bags so that we can all sleep under the stars. We know it might rain, and sometimes it does. We know a cat may sneak in, and sometimes one does. We know we may get mosquito bites and that there is no alarm system attached to the *sukkah* door. Nevertheless, we know that God is watching over us, and we go to sleep feeling happy, loved, and secure.

Living in Israel is in many ways like living in a *sukkah* all year round. We know that we are surrounded by enemies on all sides. We know that the next terror attack can happen at any time, anywhere. My children have lived through wars, heard the piercing air raid sirens, and experienced running to a bomb shelter. We have had many talks about faith in God during these times.

… it is here in the Holy Land that we can see God's majesty, experience His glory, and feel His unending love and protection.

At the same time, we are all very aware that we live in the land where, "*the eyes of the LORD your God are continually on it from the beginning of the year to its end*" (Deuteronomy 11:12). We know that He who guards Israel neither slumbers nor sleeps (Psalm 121:4). We have experienced God's providence and seen His miracles — we speak about them to our children, reflect upon them, and make sure that nothing goes unnoticed.

From the very outset, the land of Israel has been a land that requires faith in order to live. Even in biblical times, it was evident that rain in the Holy Land was not a given, and consequently, sustenance was most obviously dependent upon God. It was something that had to be prayed for. Today, we joke that God gave the nation of Israel the only sliver of land in the entire Middle East without oil! And yet, God knew exactly what He was doing when he gifted us this land that is low in natural resources but overflowing in His spirit. In the Jewish tradition, Israel is known as the land of faith, because it is only through faith and trust in God that one can live in the land, build houses, and plan for the future.

Perhaps there is no greater training ground in faith than the land of Israel, and I am so grateful that my children experience that every day of their lives. They have learned to trust God for protection. They live everyday knowing that they are the culmination of God's promises and biblical prophecy. They witness prophecy come to fruition in the streets where they walk, the people they meet, the freedom they enjoy, and the produce of the land they feast upon.

Like the *sukkah*, sometimes the rain gets in — sometimes life doesn't go the way we would like. There are plenty of times when life in Israel is challenging and scary. Yet, just as the *sukkah* also lets in the sun and provides a magnificent view of the resplendent starry nights, it is here in the Holy Land that we can see God's majesty, experience His glory, and feel His unending love and protection.

King David, the master of trusting God, wrote, *"When I said, 'My foot is slipping,' your unfailing love, LORD, supported me. When anxiety was great within me, your consolation brought me joy"* (Psalm 94:18–19). As Jesus taught his disciples in his great Sermon on the Mount, *"Therefore I tell you, do not worry about your life, what you will eat or drink; or about your body, what you will wear. Is not life more than food, and the body more than clothes? Look at the birds of the air; they do not sow or reap or store away in barns, and yet your heavenly Father feeds them. Are you not much more valuable than they?"* (Matthew 6:25–26). May we all learn to live out our faith in God each and every day, trusting Him with our very lives, knowing that He alone is *"my rock, my fortress, and my deliverer"* (Psalm 18:2).

SUKKOT IN THE
NEW TESTAMENT

As one of the three great pilgrimage festivals the Jewish people were commanded to observe, *Sukkot,* or the Festival of Tabernacles, certainly would have been observed by Jesus. In John 7, we read about Jesus going to the Festival of Tabernacles in secret because the religious leaders were already watching for him (v.11). During the weeklong festival, Jesus spent much time in the Temple, teaching the crowds and causing dissent among those who believed he was a prophet (v.40), those who believed he was the messiah (v.41), and those who believed he was a fraud (vv.44–52). It was on the final day of *Sukkot* that Jesus taught, "*Let anyone who is thirsty come to me and drink. Whoever believes in me, as Scripture has said, rivers of living water will flow from within them*" (John 7:37–38). The reference to "*living water*" echoes the very term used in Zechariah 14:8 that describes the culmination of the yearly pilgrimage of Gentiles to Jerusalem on *Sukkot* during messianic times.

FAMILY TIME — TEACHING OUR CHILDREN FAITH

1. Discuss with your family what it means to have faith in some-
    one or something. How is that kind of faith different (or simi-
    lar) to having faith in God?

2. Read the story of the four men who brought their paralyzed
    friend to Jesus for healing in Mark 2:1–12. How did the four men
    demonstrate their faith? How did Jesus respond? What does
    this story tell us about the importance of faith?

3. The author of Hebrews wrote, "*Now faith is confidence in what we
    hope for and assurance about what we do not see*" (Hebrews 11:1).
    Read some of the examples of great faith described in Chapter 11;
    discuss how each demonstrated this definition of faith.

For Parents

Yael wrote, "In the Jewish Oral Tradition, the *sukkah* is referred to
as a 'shelter of faith.' Houses rest upon strong physical foundations
and rely upon human ability. A *sukkah*, in contrast, rests on faith
alone and relies solely on God to protect the structure and the
people within it." What can you do to help your family build their
own "shelter of faith" and trust solely in God for guidance and
protection?

MEMORY VERSES

Select one of the verses below for you and your family to memorize on living with faith.

Those who know your name trust in you,
for you, LORD, have never forsaken those
who seek you. — PSALM 9:10

Trust in the LORD with all your heart
and lean not on your own understanding;
in all your ways submit to him,
and he will make your paths straight. — PROVERBS 3:5-6

"But blessed is the one who trusts in the LORD,
whose confidence is in him." — JEREMIAH 17:7

For we live by faith, not by sight. — 2 CORINTHIANS 5:7

And without faith it is impossible to please God,
because anyone who comes to him must believe
that he exists and that he rewards those who
earnestly seek him. — HEBREWS 11:6

לְדוֹר וָדוֹר

L'DOR V'DOR

PURIM

TEACHING OUR CHILDREN COURAGE

"Have I not commanded you? Be strong and
courageous. Do not be afraid; do not be
discouraged, for the LORD your God will be
with you wherever you go." — JOSHUA 1:9

"Trust yourself. Create the kind of self that you will be happy to live with all your life. Make the most of yourself by fanning the tiny, inner sparks of possibility into flames of achievement."

— *Golda Meir, (1898–1978), fourth Prime Minister of Israel, 1969–1974*

O F ALL THE VALUES I HOPE TO PASS DOWN TO MY CHILDREN, courage is one of the most important. If our children are to grow up and live the values and teachings that we have passed on to them, they will need a solid foundation of faith and courage in order to choose what is right over what is popular, and to favor what pleases God over what impresses other people. As renowned British statesman Winston Churchill said, "Courage is rightly esteemed the first of human qualities ... because it is the quality which guarantees all others." In a world that seems to have lost its moral compass, it is imperative that we teach our children how to navigate and follow a faith-based journey through life with courage and determination.

Before the Jewish people became known as the Jews, we were known as the Israelites, and before we were known by that designation, we were known as the Hebrews. The term "Hebrew" was first used to describe Abraham, who was called "Abram Ha'Ivri," "*Abram the Hebrew*," in Genesis 14:13. This term is literally translated as "Abraham, who stands on the other side." Jewish tradition teaches that Abraham earned this name because he stood apart from everyone else in the world at that time. While the culture around him believed in paganism, idolatry, hostility, and competition, Abraham taught about one loving God, morality, justice, and treating one another with kindness. It was a radically different outlook, and it was extremely unpopular.

Yet, all it took was one person who had the courage to speak the truth in spite of popular opinion, and from that flowed the three great faiths: Judaism, Christianity, and Islam. Tradition teaches that Abraham was so courageous that given the choice to renounce his faith or enter a fiery furnace, Abraham chose the latter. However, God protected Abraham, and he emerged without a single hair singed. In the Christian Bible, it was the courage of men like Peter and John that caught the attention of others and caused the early church to grow (Acts 4:13). The virtue of courage is a cornerstone of both our faiths and remains just as essential today in preserving and growing our faith communities.

Interestingly, the *Talmud* charges parents with the obligation to teach their children how to swim. This requirement demonstrates that parents have a moral and ethical responsibility to teach their children how to remain safe in dangerous situations. It has been suggested that this directive also requires that parents equip their children to deal with difficult situations even when no physical danger is present. The act of swimming demands that a person actively work to stay afloat and fight against the current that is threatening to pull him or her underwater. Likewise in life, we need to learn how to overcome challenges when they are so difficult that they threaten to "drown" us. We need to be equipped to go against the grain of society when circumstances require it. While it is always easier to "go with the flow," it is our duty to give our children the ability to swim against the current of society when necessary.

I believe that it is faith that gives us courage, and courage that gives us the confidence to do whatever it is that we are called to do. When Joshua took over the leadership of the Israelites from Moses, God repeated the same phrase to him three times in the first nine verses of the book of Joshua. God said, "*chazak V' amatz*," "*Be strong and be courageous*" (Joshua 1:6, 7, 9). As Joshua began the daunting task of conquering and settling the land of Israel — as you remember, a task believed impossible by ten of his colleagues when they spied on the land 40 years earlier — he needed courage. However, it was his unwavering faith in God that gave him the ability to act courageously and to know confidently that he would succeed in his mission. When David tasked his son Solomon with building God's great Holy Temple in Jerusalem, he said, *"Be strong and courageous, and do the work. Do not be afraid or discouraged, for the LORD God, my God, is with you"* (1 Chronicles 28:20). It was Daniel's unwavering faith in God that gave him and his friends the courage to stand against the Babylonian culture. Together, faith and courage have always advanced God's work on earth.

Courage is born out of faith — faith in God and faith in one's self, for you were created by God in the image of God.

My *Abba* (father) told me the following story that demonstrates the amazing courage that comes from deep faith. In the beginning of the 20th century, the renowned Rabbi Yosef Yitzchak Schneersohn (1880–1950) was fighting for religious freedom in communist Russia. One morning as he prayed in synagogue, three men rushed in and arrested the rabbi for his actions. Facing a council of determined men, the rabbi reaffirmed that he would not give up his religious activities. One of the agents pointed a gun at his head and said, "This little toy has made many a man change his mind!" The rabbi replied, "That little toy can only intimidate men with many gods and one world. But I have only one God and two worlds, so I am not impressed by your little toy."

As my father taught me, "He who fears One, fears none," or as King David so beautifully wrote, "*I will fear no evil, for you are with me*" (Psalm 23:4).

———

Courage is born out of faith — faith in God and faith in one's self, for you were created by God in the image of God. One of my father's favorite things to do when my sisters and I were young was to read books to us — and not just any books, but books with messages that would inspire us to believe in ourselves. Two bedtime classics in our home were *The Little Engine That Could,* by Watty Piper, and *The Value of Believing in Yourself: The Story of Louis Pasteur*, by Spencer Johnson. For many of us, *The Little Engine That Could* is a childhood staple. The delightful words of Watty Piper introduced me to that intrepid and spunky little blue engine who, in spite of being small and quite ordinary, was able to pull a large cargo over a steep mountain all because she kept repeating, "I think I can, I think I can, I think I can." *The Value of Believing in Yourself*, about the well-known 19th-century French chemist who discovered the vaccine for the deadly rabies virus, told of Pasteur's persistent and constant refrain: "I believe I can, I believe I can." The heroes of my bedtime stories were successful in accomplishing things great and small because of the one thing they had in common — both believed in themselves, and consequently had the courage to pursue goals others thought impossible to achieve.

Having this idea reinforced nearly every night provided an indelible message that I could achieve whatever it is that I put my mind to. However, this message was carefully balanced by the idea that I could do nothing without God. Taken together, my father taught my sisters and me the invaluable lesson that with God in our lives, we could do anything. It is a lesson that has served both my sisters and me well over the years.

If God brought me to it, God would get me through it. With such knowledge, how can we not have courage?

My parents were well aware that they were raising three girls who would become women in a world that tends to give men the advantage. It was important to them to instill within us the idea that we were just as capable as our male counterparts, and that as women, we have our own unique gifts to contribute to society. They emphasized the morning blessing recited by women daily in Jewish prayer, which thanks God for "making me according to His Will." They taught us that God created us with every tool and talent we would ever need to accomplish His work. My parents filled us with courage and confidence on a daily basis that we could meet any challenge and reach every goal. They helped me believe that anything I would be called to do would be something that I would undoubtedly be able to accomplish. If God brought me to it, God would get me through it. With such knowledge, how can we not have courage?

——

As a lifelong champion of women, my father felt particularly connected to the holiday of *Purim*, when we celebrate Queen Esther, the heroine who saved the Jews. According to the book of Esther, the Jewish people were destined for annihilation due to the evil machinations of the wicked Haman, but with the help of God working behind the scenes, Queen Esther courageously risked her life to save her people.

Most are probably familiar with this story that takes place after the destruction of the First Temple in Jerusalem while the Jewish people lived in Persian exile under the rule of King Xerxes. As the story goes, after the king had banished his first wife, he looked for a new wife and chose Esther, a young Jewish orphan. Under the direction of her Uncle Mordecai, Esther did not reveal her Jewish identity. While Esther was queen, an evil man named Haman plotted to kill all the Jewish people, and through a series of well-placed lies and deceptions, was granted permission by the king to do so. Haman drew lots to determine the day that the genocide would take place — the 14th day of the month of *Adar*.

Mordecai informed Esther of the looming threat and instructed her to go before the king and beg for mercy for her people. Esther, however, was hesitant. She knew that anyone who appeared before the king without being summoned would be put to death unless the king favored them. But Mordecai encouraged Esther to do her duty with these stirring words, *"And who knows but that you have come to your royal position for such a time as this?"* (Esther 4:14). Esther accepted the mission, requesting that the nation of Israel fast on her behalf, and ultimately succeeded in saving her people.

… Esther was so consumed by fear and weak from fasting that it took two angels to hold up her body and one to hold up her head.

Today, *Purim*, which means "lots" in ancient Babylonian and recalls the lots that Haman drew to determine the day of destruction for the Jews, is celebrated on the 14th day of the Hebrew month *Adar.* The day before *Purim* is known as the "Fast of Esther," and Jews fast in remembrance of the original fast requested by Esther. On *Purim* itself, the book of Esther is read, a feast is held, and the directives of Mordecai and Esther to give gifts to the needy and send food to friends in order to increase camaraderie are fulfilled (Esther 9:20–22). Another prominent custom of the day that has evolved over the years is to dress up in costumes in order to demonstrate that things are not as they seem. While the hand of God is evident throughout the story of Esther, His name is never mentioned in the text itself. On *Purim,* we remember that even though God often seems hidden or disguised in our lives, He is always there.

———

U.S. President Franklin D. Roosevelt once said, "Courage is not the absence of fear but rather the assessment that there is something more important than fear." In the *Purim* story, Esther is a shining example of courage mainly because she was also the victim of intense fear.

For most of the story, Esther was a passive character. She was raised by Mordecai, taken against her will to the palace, forced to marry King Xerxes, and then followed the rules set out by Mordecai regarding her conduct in the palace. When confronted with the task of saving the Jews, her immediate reaction was to reject it, explaining that *"for any man or woman who approaches the king in the inner court without being summoned the king has but one law: that they be put to death unless the king extends the gold scepter to them and spares their lives"* (Esther 4:11). Esther, rightfully so, feared for her life.

However, once Mordecai made his case, Esther rose to the occasion and proclaimed, *"And if I perish, I perish"* (Esther 4:16). In that moment, she realized that there was something much larger at stake — the very life and continuity of the entire Jewish nation. This was the turning point for both Esther and the Jews. For the first time, she became assertive, in spite of her fear, and commanded Mordecai to call a three-day fast on her behalf. On the third day, she approached the king. According to Jewish tradition, Esther was so consumed by fear and weak from fasting that it took two angels to hold up her body and one to hold up her head. When she faced the king, her life was spared; however, she did not yet have the courage to make her request.

Esther's fast brought about salvation, and her courage laid the groundwork for God to save His people.

Instead, Esther invited the king and her enemy, Haman, to a feast where she planned to present her plea to the king once he was in a good mood. However, even with the king's promise to grant her up to half of the kingdom, Esther postponed her request and invited the pair to yet another feast. Finally, at the second feast, Esther revealed her identity, asked for the salvation of her people, and succeeded in saving the Jews. The 14th day of *Adar*, which was expected to be a day of utter horror for the Jewish nation, became a day of great joy and celebration.

I always found it curious that the Jewish people commemorate the Fast of Esther the day before *Purim*, the 13th of *Adar*, because

Scripture tells us that the couriers announced Haman's evil edict on the 13th day of *Nissan* (Esther 3:12). The Fast of Esther then was held during the middle of *Nissan*, which is actually Passover! The day chosen through lots to obliterate the Jews was actually 11 months later on the 14th of *Adar*. Moreover, during the time when the terrible decree was declared and Esther succeeded in saving the Jews, there were two fasts — one initiated by the people who reacted to Haman's initial decree by *"fasting, weeping and wailing"* (Esther 4:3), and the one that Esther called for before approaching the king (Esther 4:16). Why do we only commemorate Esther's fast?

According to Jewish teachings, while the story of *Purim* is about God's providence behind the scenes, it is also about the importance of each individual person stepping up with courage to fulfill his or her God-given role. We can only fully appreciate the salvation that took place on *Purim* if we first appreciate the courage it took for one young orphan girl to step out in faith and bravely save her people. Esther's fast brought about salvation, and her courage laid the groundwork for God to save His people.

When my parents read me all those self-affirming books and taught me to hold Esther as a role model, I had no idea that these teachings would be essential to overcoming the greatest challenge I have ever encountered.

In February 2019, I unexpectedly lost my father. Looking back now it seems that it was divine providence that he passed away on the first day of the month of *Adar* — the Hebrew month in which we celebrate *Purim* and a month in which we are to be joyful. At the time, I noted that it was fitting that my father passed away in the month of *Adar* because the events commemorated during this month matched his life's work, as he brought so much joy and salvation to the Jewish people. Now I see that *Adar* not only fit my father's life story, but also my own. It was the story of Esther that saw me through those first difficult weeks and months after my loss. I realized during those first months after my father's death that just as God had prepared Esther for *"such a time as this,"* He had been preparing me for that very moment.

All I needed to fulfill this role was already within me; I just needed the courage and faith to push forward.

To me, my father was not only a loving, supportive, and wise parent, he was also my leader and mentor. I had the privilege of working side-by-side with him at the *International Fellowship of Christians and Jews (The Fellowship)* for more than 16 years. Suddenly, he was no longer there, and my world had turned upside down. While my father had begun preparing me to take over leadership at the organization that he founded and built, we both had expected the transition to take place a few years later and with him by my side to guide me. However, with this unexpected turn of events, I became president of *The Fellowship* overnight. I barely had internalized my father's death when I became one of the young-est women to lead any comparable nonprofit organization in the United States.

> Perhaps more than any teaching, watching me go through this challenge and mustering the courage to go forward taught my children the value of faith-based courage.

My father's shoes are enormous ones to fill. Yet, his teachings and guidance have reassured me. I could hear him say, "Perhaps you have reached this position for such a time as this." I drew on the lessons that I learned as a child from my father and mother — that if God had brought me to this position, I absolutely could do it. All I needed to fulfill this role was already within me; I just needed the courage and faith to push forward. God was most certainly with me, just as He had been with Esther and all the other courageous heroes of the Bible.

The year that followed was an incredible journey, and it was one on which I brought my children along with me. They, too, were hurting; they had lost a beloved *saba*, a grandfather, someone who had been such a presence in their young lives. And they, too, had to deal with the reality of me taking on a more demanding position outside the home.

We started a tradition that we upheld throughout the year following my father's death. Every Sabbath eve as I lit the traditional *Shabbat* candles, we lit a commemoration candle in memory of my *Abba* and their *Saba*, which lasted all week long until the next Sabbath. When we lit that candle, we would share a memory about my father and their grandfather, and encourage each other through our loss. It was during this time that I shared with my children my thoughts and feelings about, literally, sitting in my father's chair and taking over his position. I would share the many challenges that I faced each week, and how the lessons I learned from my father helped me through. I shared how my faith was strengthened as I felt God's presence and love with every difficult step I took.

Perhaps more than any teaching, watching me go through this challenge and mustering the courage to go forward taught my children the value of faith-based courage. What was at first scary, unknown, and intimidating became familiar and even a great source of joy in our home as we witnessed *The Fellowship* not only continue to function, but also to grow in the months after my father's death.

As much as I pray that my children encounter as little sadness and struggle in their lives as possible, I know that God sends all of us challenges — challenges tailored to our innate abilities, weaknesses, and life purpose. I believe that the amount of courage we bring with us when we are met with such challenges will greatly determine our ability to surmount them, or God forbid, to give up in despair. By sharing my experiences with my children, I hope that if they ever question their ability to fulfill God's plan for their lives, they will look back on their mother, just as I looked back to Esther, my ancestor, and know that if she can do it, so can they. They will know that while God gives us burdens, He will bring them through it if they, like Joshua, are *"to be strong and be courageous."*

PURIM IN THE NEW TESTAMENT

Purim is not mentioned in the New Testament, as might be expected since it is not one of the three pilgrimage holy days that required the Israelites to go to Jerusalem. Rather, *Purim* was observed locally. Some biblical scholars believe the feast mentioned in John 5:1 — *"Some time later, Jesus went up to Jerusalem for one of the Jewish festivals"* — is referring to *Purim* because it is not named and because of the timing. However, others dispute that because of Jesus' presence in Jerusalem, signifying it might have been a pilgrimage holiday. Regardless, the courage of an Esther can be found throughout the pages of the New Testament — in a young woman from Nazareth obediently bearing a child out-of-wedlock (Luke 1:26–38); the women who went to the cross, while the other disciples fled in fear (John 19:25); to Peter and John defying the religious leaders to preach about Jesus (Acts 5:17–41).

FAMILY TIME — TEACHING OUR CHILDREN TO BE COURAGEOUS

1. As a family, share a time when you had to decide whether to speak out against the popular opinion or go along with the crowd. What did you decide? How did you feel about making that decision? What was the outcome?

2. Read the story of Peter and John in Acts 4:12–31. What were they risking by speaking out? What was their response to the religious leaders? What did the believers pray for in vv.24–30? What do these stories teach us about courage and faith?

3. Christian theologian and preacher Billy Graham once wrote, "Courage is contagious. When a brave man takes a stand, the spines of others are often stiffened." Discuss where you have witnessed this. How might you put courage into practice daily?

For Parents

Yael wrote, "The heroes of my bedtime stories were successful in accomplishing things great and small because of the one thing they had in common — both believed in themselves, and consequently had the courage to pursue goals others thought impossible to achieve." Consider selecting books about courageous heroes to read with your children.

MEMORY VERSES

Select one of the verses below on courage for you and your family to memorize.

"Have I not commanded you? Be strong and
courageous. Do not be afraid; do not be
discouraged, for the LORD your God will be
with you wherever you go." — JOSHUA 1:9

Be strong and take heart,
all you who hope in the LORD. — PSALM 31:24

So do not fear, for I am with you;
do not be dismayed, for I am your God.
I will strengthen you and help you;
I will uphold you with my righteous
right hand. — ISAIAH 41:10

Be on your guard; stand firm in the faith; be courageous;
be strong. — 1 CORINTHIANS 16:13

Finally, be strong in the Lord and in his mighty
power. — EPHESIANS 6:10

L'DOR V'DOR

TZEDAKAH

TEACHING OUR CHILDREN GENEROSITY

There will always be poor people in the land. Therefore I
command you to be openhanded toward your fellow
Israelites who are poor and needy in your land.

— DEUTERONOMY 15:11

"If I am not for myself, who will
be for me? If I am only for myself,
what am I? And if not now, when?"

*— Hillel the Elder, (110 BCE-10 CE), first-century Jewish religious
leader and scholar*

G ROWING UP, I LOVED TAKING PHOTOGRAPHS WITH MY
father's camera. To this day, I cherish the pictures I took on
our family vacations. When disposable cameras came out, and my
parents bought me one to take on a school trip, I enthusiastically
took pictures of everything and everyone. Today, as we well know,
cameras are much more available, as nearly every mobile phone has
one; I still marvel at the ability to capture special moments with the
touch of a button. Yet, while I am thankful for the modern miracle
of photography, I have noticed a trend, especially among children,
that concerns me.

Our children are growing up in what has been dubbed "the
selfie generation." Most photos that kids take these days are of

themselves. The accessibility of digital cameras, the ease of taking self-portraits, and the rise of social media have all led to the popularity of "selfies," the new term for modern-day digital self-portraits. From selfies taken from space to comedian Ellen DeGeneres taking a group selfie at an Oscar ceremony, photographic gratification is rampant on the internet and social media. Personally, I take plenty of selfies with the intention of sharing my life in the Holy Land with people of faith around the world. However, as many sociologists have noticed, the word selfie has taken on a meaning that goes far beyond the object of the camera lens. It's not just in photos that children are often the focus — it can extend into their lives.

The selfie culture turns people's focus onto themselves — how they look, how many "likes" they get on social media, what kind of clothing they wear, how much fun they have, and so on. What started out as a harmless, fun activity has now been linked to growing rates of depression — and certainly an increase of narcissism. The great irony, of course, is that focusing on ourselves does not make us happier; rather it robs us of our joy. In contrast, the Bible teaches us about another, more genuine source of joy. Solomon, the wisest man to ever walk the earth, wrote, *"he who has mercy on the poor, happy is he"* (Proverbs 14:21 NKJV). It is giving to others that truly brings us joy.

The challenge for parents today is teaching our children to take the focus off themselves and turn the camera around so that they can see others. We need to teach our children to see the people around them. First and foremost this includes their friends, their siblings, their parents, and their teachers. But it extends beyond that to the people they encounter in daily life: the bus driver, the janitor, the widow, the orphan, the homeless person on the street corner. Only when our children begin to see others' intrinsic value and suffering can they begin to understand how they can help others.

Hillel the Elder, a *Torah* scholar in the first century BCE, said, "If I am not for myself, who will be for me? If I am only for myself, what am I? And if not now, when?" Essentially, he taught that while we certainly have a responsibility to take care of our own needs, we also have an equally important obligation to help others *now*, not at some later date when it's more convenient or when we have more resources. As parents, we absolutely should teach our children to take care of themselves so that they can become independent people. But it is also our job as people of faith to teach them to be givers and to lovingly share what they have with those in need.

———

From a young age, my parents were very clear about the importance of giving to the needy. As soon as we had any source of our own money, they taught my sisters and me the biblical principle of the tithe — giving ten percent of our money to charity (Leviticus 27:30; Numbers 18:26). So when we earned babysitting money, we automatically set aside a tenth of what we made for charitable giving.

However, my parents were not interested in merely teaching us to give our money to charity. Their ultimate goal was for us to become generous people — people who looked past our own desires and concerns and saw the needs and challenges of others. There was no better way to teach us this lesson than through their living example.

I learned from my parents that giving comes in many forms and that a generous person gives in all ways.

I remember one particular night, as I lay in bed, there was a knock on our front door. My father was sitting on the edge of my bed, singing me to sleep, while my mother was busy putting my sisters to bed. My father got up from our nighttime routine to answer the door, finding a complete stranger who he immediately realized was there to ask for charity. This was actually very common in Jewish communities where the needy felt they could ask for help from fellow Jews. Most people handed the beggars some money, wished them a good night, and got on with their busy schedules.

But not my parents.

My parents would always invite the needy man or woman inside our home, sit them at our dining room table, and serve them a cup of coffee and a piece of cake. One or both of my parents would sit with our guest and listen intently to their story, hearing their problems, sometimes discussing an idea from the Bible. Only afterward did they give whatever we could afford to the person and send them on their way. My father always said, "It's harder to ask for help than to give help. If a person asks, we must give, and we have to make them feel as comfortable as possible in an extremely uncomfortable situation."

This night was no different, and the man was welcomed into our home as an honored guest. My parents put bedtime on hold so that they could tend to our guest, and only after he left did they resume where they had left off. The fact that my parents interrupted our nightly routine for the sake of an unexpected stranger in need left an indelible impression on me. It taught me that helping a person in need, even a complete stranger, is of utmost importance, and requires our immediate attention. Not later. Not the next day. Now.

The Jewish concept of *tzedakah* beckons us to understand that charity is an act that profoundly effects both the giver and the receiver.

My father behaved similarly when we came across needy people on the street. He smiled, said hello, and struck up a conversation with complete strangers who most people would overlook and bypass. I watched homeless people transform in seconds as they went from looking dejected to energized with life and light as my father spoke with them.

I learned from my parents that giving comes in many forms and that a generous person gives in all ways. Yes, my parents gave their money, but they also gave generously of their time, their effort, their attention, their compassion, and their love. Most importantly, they gave joyfully with a full heart.

Giving charity is a defining characteristic of Jewish life. In Hebrew, the word for charity, *tzedakah*, has a very different meaning than the ideas we typically associate with the word charity, described in the dictionary as "the voluntary giving of help, typically in the form of money, to those in need." Most people of faith associate charity with words like mercy, kindness, and compassion. However, the word *tzedakah* in Hebrew comes from two root words: *tzedek*, which means "justice," and *kah*, a reference to God's name. Taken together, *tzedakah* means "the justice of God," and is most accurately translated as "righteous giving." In that sense, giving charity is primarily an act of righteousness, a sacred obligation, and a necessary act in our service to God. God says, "*The silver is mine and the gold is mine*" (Haggai 2:8). Everything that we possess — from the wealth that we attain, to the talents and circumstances that allowed us to acquire it — are gifts from God. God has given us all that we have so that we might use our resources appropriately. So when we give to the needy, in essence, we return to God what is truly His in the first place.

Tzedakah is practiced in the Jewish faith all year long, and ideally, every day. Jewish homes, schools, and synagogues have at least one special receptacle called a *tzedakah* box where people can give charity. Many women and girls give *tzedakah* just before lighting the Sabbath candles on Friday before sunset. Charity is a notable feature of our holidays as well, such as during the High Holy Days when giving to the needy is said to sweeten God's judgement, or on Passover when the *seder* meal begins with an invitation to all who are hungry. On *Purim*, we are explicitly directed to give "*gifts to the poor*" (Esther 9:22). In addition, people often give *tzedakah* as a way to commemorate a loved one who has passed, or to honor the living.

As mentioned previously, Jews are obligated to give away ten percent of their earnings, a practice known as tithing (Leviticus 27:30), which is observed by many Christians as well. Giving *tzedakah* is regarded so highly that it is considered one of the few acts that is "equal to fulfilling the entire *Torah*." In other words, giving charity is an essential part of the purpose of life. As the apostle Paul, raised and educated as a Jew, wrote to the church at Corinth, "*And now abideth faith, hope, charity, these three; but the greatest of these is charity*" (1 Corinthians 13:13 KJV).

The Jewish concept of *tzedakah* beckons us to understand that charity is an act that profoundly effects both the giver and the receiver. The receiver experiences the blessing of the gift and the subsequent change to his or her physical status, while the giver receives spiritual blessings. It says in the *Talmud,* the written compilation of the Jewish Oral Tradition, "More than the wealthy person does for the poor, the poor does for the wealthy person." As Solomon wrote, *"The generous will themselves be blessed, for they share their food with the poor"* (Proverbs 22:9; see also 14:21 and 19:17). And Jesus taught in the Christian Bible, *"And if anyone gives even a cup of cold water to one of these little ones who is my disciple, truly I tell you, that person will certainly not lose their reward"* (Matthew 10:42). Clearly, there is a reward for those who bless the less fortunate.

The Bible says, *"There will always be poor people in the land. Therefore I command you to be openhanded toward your fellow Israelites who are poor and needy in your land"* (Deuteronomy 15:11). The Jewish understanding of this verse is that there will always be people in need of our charity, not because God desires the suffering of poor people, but because He wants us to become generous human beings. God's heart for the poor, the widowed, and the orphan becomes abundantly clear in the many laws He gave to the people of Israel as they established their new godly nation. In Leviticus 25:35, He commanded the people, *"'If any of your fellow Israelites become poor and are unable to support themselves among* you, help them as you would a foreigner and stranger, so they can continue to live among you." He told them to be "openhanded" to those in need (Deuteronomy 15:8) for the righteous "are always generous and lend freely" (Psalm 37:26). If that is God's heart, it should certainly be ours, too.

When we see the needy as beloved family, how could we not give willingly, generously, and with love?

There is an axiom in Judaism that says, "The heart follows the actions." This means that what we do effects how we feel. This is why giving is an obligation, not an option. God commanded us to give to the poor no matter how we may feel because the more we give, the more we feel like giving and not the other way around. Interestingly, the Hebrew word for love, *ahava,* is rooted in the word *hav,* which denotes "giving." This teaches us that love is a byproduct of giving. The biblical directive to "*love your neighbor*" (Leviticus 19:18) is best fulfilled through giving. Echoing this directive in his famous Sermon on the Mount, Jesus taught, "*Give to the one who asks you, and do not turn away from the one who wants to borrow from you*" (Matthew 5:42).

Rabbi Israel Salanter, a 19th-century scholar, taught: "Someone else's material needs are my spiritual responsibility." We develop our souls by helping others fill their physical needs. Judaism maintains that it is better to give a smaller amount of charity regularly than to give one large gift and refrain from giving year-round. Just as we need to exercise a muscle regularly in order to make it stronger, we need to give consistently in order to fully develop the trait of generosity. By placing *tzedakah* boxes in our homes and places of gathering, we give ourselves the opportunity to give charity every day. The box serves as a daily reminder that there are people in need of our assistance, and provides a way for us to do our part to help every day.

The goal for us is to give consistently and generously, but giving our hard-earned money can be difficult. Even with generous hearts, our heads might worry that we will not have enough for ourselves if we give our resources away. However, God promised that, "*Those who give to the poor will lack nothing ...*" (Proverbs 28:27). In addition, God declared that when we give *tzedakah*, not only will He "pay us back," He will increase us. "*Bring the whole tithe into the storehouse, that there may be food in my house,*" God said. He promised, "*Test me in this ... and see if I will not throw open the floodgates of heaven and pour out so much blessing that there will not be room enough to store it*" (Malachi 3:10). In the Christian Bible, Paul taught, "*And God is able to bless you abundantly, so that in all things at all times, having all that you need, you will abound in every good work ... You will be enriched in every way so that you can be generous on every occasion, and through us your generosity will result in thanksgiving to God*" (2 Corinthians 9:8; 11).

Ultimately, generosity comes naturally when we learn to see the poor as our brethren. In Judaism, we note that every time Scripture commands us to give to the poor, the word "brother" appears as well. This teaches that we must see the needy as our own family members. Just as we would never turn our backs on our loved ones, we must never close our hearts to those who are also the children of God, our brothers and sisters in the family of God. When we see the needy as beloved family, how could we not give willingly, generously, and with love?

In my home, I try to pass on to my children the same sense of generosity that I learned from my own parents by caring for those in need with genuine concern, respect, and love. My intention is to teach my children to give in the fullest sense — of their money, their time, their attention, and their empathy.

To that end, my husband and I bring our children with us once or twice a month to help distribute aid to needy Jews around Israel. In addition, we have multiple *tzedakah* boxes placed around our home in order to encourage giving regularly and spontaneously. We also place money in our *tzedakah* box before lighting *Shabbat* candles on Friday evening. On *Shabbat*, we invite anyone without a place to eat to come share a meal in our home with our family. We involve our children as much as we can in charitable giving and efforts so that they can experience firsthand the joy and fulfillment that giving brings to both the giver and the receiver.

Over the years, we have met and befriended needy people in nearby cities, who then became parts of our lives. One such man, David, started out as a stranger we met on the streets of Jerusalem, but as we got to know him, he became a beloved friend. Once we took the time to hear his story, it became clear that David was a holy man who had fallen on hard times. He had spent years studying the Bible with some of Jerusalem's most respected rabbis, so every encounter with him became a Bible lesson for us. When his daughter got married, we helped with the wedding; when she had her first child, we brought diapers; and when David died, we went to his funeral. We held him up in our home as an example of faith and devotion, kindness, and wisdom. Yes, we gave David money, but more importantly, we gave him respect and dignity. Both are life-giving.

I knew my children had absorbed at least part of this lesson when we were driving to school late one day and my three-year-old insisted that we stop in order to thank the street sweeper. Thankfully I realized the educational value in the moment, so I pulled over and rolled down the car windows. My son thanked the man for keeping our streets clean, which put a huge smile on both of their faces. We were continuing on to school, when my son again insisted that we stop and return to the man. "We didn't ask him his name!" my son said. "How can we really thank him if we don't even know his name?" Again, I realized the importance of this encounter, so I backed up and pulled over to the street sweeper again. We asked his name and learned that he was an Ethiopian Jew who had made *aliyah* (immigrated to Israel) less than a decade earlier. We brought him some coffee and listened to his story.

As we finally got back on our way to school, I remembered how my father used to serve coffee to the beggars who came to our door when I was a little girl. I thought about how he had watched his own father — for whom my son is named — welcome countless guests into his home as the rabbi of his community. In that one brief encounter, spurred on by the insistence of my three-year-old son, I could see the chain of generations stretching all the way back to Abraham, who taught the world about kindness, continuing far beyond my own family. I knew then that there is no greater accomplishment than being a strong link in that chain, drawing on the immense strength and wisdom of those who came before us and passing it on to the next generation and all generations to come. *L'dor v'dor.*

TZEDAKAH IN THE NEW TESTAMENT

The concept of righteous giving, *tzedakah*, and helping the poor can be found throughout the New Testament's teachings. On numerous occasions, Jesus taught his followers to take care of the poor, *"But now as for what is inside you — be generous to the poor, and everything will be clean for you"* (Luke 11:41). When a leading ruler who had faithfully kept God's commandments asked Jesus what he must do to inherit eternal life, Jesus replied, *"You still lack one thing. Sell everything you have and give to the poor, and you will have treasure in heaven"* (Luke 18:22). Indeed, giving to the poor was a characteristic of the early church: *"They sold property and possessions to give to anyone who had need"* (Acts 2:45), so that *"there were no needy persons among them"* (Acts 4:34). As Jesus taught, *"And if anyone gives even a cup of cold water to one of these little ones who is my disciple, truly I tell you, that person will certainly not lose their reward"* (Matthew 10:42).

FAMILY TIME — TEACHING OUR CHILDREN GENEROSITY

1. In Acts 20:35, the apostle Paul quotes Jesus as saying, *"It is more blessed to give than to receive."* Share an experience when you found this to be true.

2. Read the parable of the sheep and the goats in Matthew 25:31–46. What were the righteous rewarded for doing? Why were the "goats" punished? How does this lesson impact your family's giving habits?

3. Christian author Amy Carmichael wrote, "You can give without loving, but you cannot love without giving." As a family, discuss what you think this means. What role does love have in giving to others? How does this fit with Paul's description of love in 1 Corinthians 13?

For Parents

Yael wrote, "My husband and I bring our children with us once or twice a month to help distribute aid to needy Jews around Israel. In addition, we have multiple *tzedakah* boxes placed around our home in order to encourage giving regularly and spontaneously." In what ways can you provide your children with regular opportunities for giving or helping others?

MEMORY VERSES

Select one of the verses below on generosity for you and your family to memorize.

> *Give generously to them and do so without a grudging*
>   *heart; then because of this the LORD your God will*
>   *bless you in all your work and in everything you*
>   *put your hand to.* — DEUTERONOMY 15:10

> *Good will come to those who are generous and lend freely,*
>   *who conduct their affairs with justice.* — PSALM 112:5

> *Whoever is kind to the poor lends to the LORD,*
>   *and he will reward them for what they have done.*
>   — PROVERBS 19:17

> *"Give to the one who asks you, and do not turn away from*
>   *the one who wants to borrow from you."*
>   — MATTHEW 5:42

> *Command them to do good, to be rich in good*
>   *deeds, and to be generous and willing*
>   *to share.* — 1 TIMOTHY 6:18